Tales of Old Nottinghamshire

Other counties in this series include:

Avon
Bedfordshire
Berkshire
Buckinghamshire
Cambridgeshire
Devon
East Anglia
Essex
Gloucestershire
Hampshire
Herefordshire
Hertfordshire
Kent
Leicestershire
Lincolnshire
Norfolk
Northamptonshire
Oxfordshire
Shropshire
Somerset
Stratford
Suffolk
Surrey
Sussex
Warwickshire
Wiltshire
Worcestershire

Tales of Old Nottinghamshire

Polly Howat

With Illustrations by Don Osmond

COUNTRYSIDE BOOKS
NEWBURY, BERKSHIRE

First published 1991

Reprinted 1999
This new edition 2011

COUNTRYSIDE BOOKS
3 Catherine Road
Newbury, Berkshire

To view our complete range of books,
please visit us at
www.countrysidebooks.co.uk

ISBN 978 1 84674 259 0

Cover designed by Peter Davies, Nautilus Design
Produced through MRM Associates Ltd., Reading
Typeset by Wessex Press Design & Print Ltd., Warminster
Printed by Information Press, Oxford

For Robert and Phyllis Howat

Acknowledgements

With grateful thanks to the staff of the Local Studies Department, Nottinghamshire County Library; the Nottinghamshire Local History Association; J. G. Staley Esq, C.Eng, M.I.Mech.E; Mr Jim Worgan, Keeper of Collelctions, Chatterley Whitfield Mining Museum.

Contents

CONTENTS

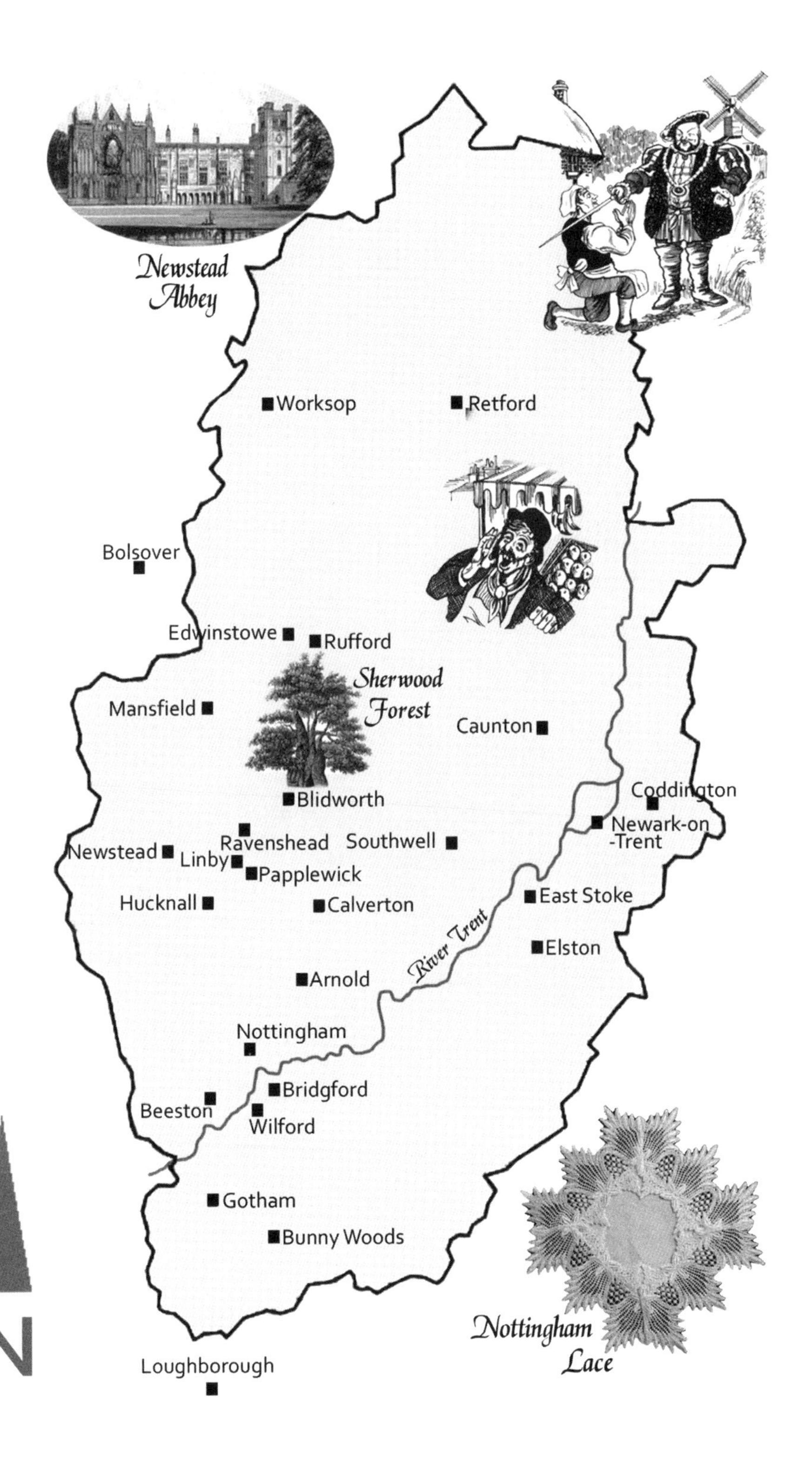

Newstead Abbey
Worksop
Retford
Bolsover
Edwinstowe
Rufford
Sherwood Forest
Mansfield
Caunton
Blidworth
Coddington
Newark-on-Trent
Ravenshead
Southwell
Newstead
Linby
Papplewick
Hucknall
Calverton
East Stoke
River Trent
Elston
Arnold
Nottingham
Bridgford
Beeston
Wilford
Gotham
Bunny Woods
Nottingham Lace
N
Loughborough

NOTTINGHAM
20 M.

The Nottingham Goose Fair

THE Goose Fair, which is held in October each year dates back to the 13th century.

In those days the Nottingham Fair was definitely the poor relation of the one held at Lenton Priory, which was a major event lasting twelve days, starting on the Feast of St Martin, 11th November. However, as Nottingham gradually expanded into a major industrialised area, its fair superseded Lenton's.

Until the end of the Middle Ages most trade conducted in this country and with foreign merchants was undertaken at fairs. Foreigners were restricted from selling in chartered towns so fairs were ideal venues, where money earned from their sales was used to purchase goods for export.

At the major fairs booths were set out in 'streets' such as Booksellers Row, Cloth Row or Fair, Tanners Row, Skinners Row and similar. In addition there was always a large Horse Fair. Not all traders could afford the luxury of cover and hawked their wares from back packs. They were prohibited from walking round making sales as this would have made it difficult for the fair owners to collect their rents.

It seems that the term 'Goose Fair' first appeared in 1541 and there are various apocryphal tales which claim to give the origins of the name. For instance there is a story told in ballad form, wherein a widower who reared his one son in total seclusion from women, took the lad to Nottingham Fair when he reached the age of majority. On seeing women for the first time the boy enquired: 'Father, what are these?' 'Birds,' said the flustered father, 'they're called Geese!' Word got out about the lad's first experience of women and the fair became known as the Goose Fair!

Another old story tells of an angler who was fishing in the river Trent, a mile or two out of Nottingham. He felt a tugging at his line and jerked it high into the air, with a good-sized pike caught on the hook. A wild goose happened to be flying overhead, grabbed the fish and took the angler with him. When the bird flew over Nottingham Market Place — the old venue of the fair — he dropped his booty of man, fish and tackle. The fisherman got up, unharmed, and to celebrate his good fortune a holiday was proclaimed.

A more plausible reason for the name is the fact that thousands of geese were driven up from the Lincolnshire Fens and even parts of Norfolk, to be sold in Nottingham's Market Place at Michaelmastide. The birds had to walk long distances to reach Nottingham and so the gooseherds who drove the flocks would make them walk through alternate patches of wet tar and sand to preserve their feet. In effect the tar and sand mixture acted as little marching boots for the birds, who could easily manage ten miles a day. Obviously when they reached their final destination they had to have a good rest and plenty of food to regain the weight they had lost in their travels, although they would have grazed on the fields en route to Nottingham.

To eat a goose on Michaelmas Day was once considered by Nottinghamshire folk to be very lucky, for as the saying goes:

'He who eats goose on Michaelmas Day,
Shan't money lack his debts to pay.'

It was also customary for landlords to receive presents from their tenants of a goose, which at that time of the year was at its perfection, having liberally grazed on the stubble fields.

Although goose was the prime commodity at the old fairs, cheese was another important factor. In about 1766 the farmers increased the price per pound by one third of that charged at the previous fair, thereby demanding from 28 shillings to 30 shillings a hundredweight. The 'Great Cheese Riot' ensued. Cheeses were hurled at the cheesemongers, whose stalls were ransacked and plundered. The mayor tried to cool tempers but ended up being knocked out by a huge cheese which was aimed straight at him. A great number of cheeses were rolled down Wheeler Gate and Peek Lane and matters got so out of control that the dragoons were summoned. The riot was quelled, but not before blood had been shed. One man named William Eggleston, while guarding some stock, was killed on the spot by the fire of a dragoon and others received serious injuries. Although a lot of people were arrested they were eventually released.

At one time you could buy almost anything at the fair, even wives were auctioned off! This was a common occurrence at many fairs throughout the country, when the womenfolk were put up for sale, each being obliged to wear a horse's collar.

The Horse Fair was also an important part of the event and the yearling ponies, which were brought from as far away as the New Forest, Wales and the Lake District, always sold well. Often the sellers 'oiled the wheels of commerce' by supplying beer to dithering customers to help them make up their minds. An article appeared in the *Nottingham Journal* in 1901 concerning a coal man who took his ancient horse called Bob to the fair to exchange it for a better nag. Whilst tipsy he purchased a horse called Phillip, who was 'worth 50 guineas', for just £20, with poor old Bob thrown in to clinch the bargain. When he got home and eventually sobered up he discovered that he had bought back his original almost worthless horse, which now had a new name and painted feet.

On 5th May 1840 the railway line linking Nottingham with Leicester was opened. Over the years the rail network was extended and this helped swell the number of people who flocked to the fair. Before the turn of the century it was estimated that the railway was responsible for bringing in some 58,000 people during the event.

The train also brought in the fantastic Bostock & Wombwell Menagerie which was one of the highlights of the fair. Weeks before the Goose Fair most children made sure that parents and neighbours had jobs to be done and errands run for a farthing or a halfpenny so they could spend their earnings over those three glorious days.

Most had to be content with just a little money and a few treats, but they still enjoyed the hurly-burly of that time. They inhaled the smell and soaked up the sound of the giant traction engines which disgorged billows of steam from their fiery bellies. Young girls screamed and swooned into the arms of their sweethearts. Squeals and giggles also came from many shadowy areas, for the Goose Fair had a reputation for its 'slap and tickle'. Even more so when it moved to The Forest with its good covering of trees and bushes! Many young women went home with permanent souvenirs.

There was an abundance of food, such as hot mushy peas wiped up with 'more gravy an da chunk of bread' (sic). Also popular were Grantham Gingerbread, brandy snaps, cockles and whelks, and toffee apples. Who could resist those delicious smells which permeated the cool autumn air, especially the chip stalls which sold their finger-burning delicacies in 'paper boats'.

There were always freaks to be gawped at in their booths, like the bearded lady and a very tall chap who looked like a lamp post and was sometimes accompanied by his two midget friends. There were gentle rides and fearsome ones such as the 'steamboat', which swayed back and forth to dizzy heights and agonising dips. This was where the bigger boys congregated on the Sunday just before the amusements were dismantled, and searched for the coppers which had fallen out of people's pockets as they flew through the air.

Besides lots of rides and amusements, other attractions included boxing booths where you could pay the price and challenge the 'pro'. If you survived three rounds you won ten shillings. There was a Wild West Show, a reptile exhibition, and trading stalls which spread out into the town. To a child brought up to expect little, these three days were like Christmas and your birthday rolled into one.

The most exciting, and expensive, time to visit the fair was at ten thirty on the Saturday night, one and a half hours before closing time. The place was so packed you could hardly move, but the atmosphere was electrifying.

In 1928 the Goose Fair moved from the Market Place to a much larger site at The Forest. The old venue was needed for redevelopment. A new extended civic centre, to be known as the Parliament Building, was scheduled for this site, along with adjacent offices and shops. It is said that one lunch time in 1927 when the builders were working on the foundations, suddenly a huge army of rats, lead by a massive King Rat, came out of the diggings, walked across Slab Square and up King Street to where the post office used to be. The column of rats was so long that it stopped the trams.

Of course the geese have long ceased to waddle their way in their makeshift foot gear along the poor roads and mud tracks. Indeed a goose at the Goose Fair now has quite a different meaning! Neither is the bird any longer traditional Michaelmas food. The combustion engine has killed off the need for a Horse Fair, but what was once described as 'The Finest Market Place in England' has survived and is now a pleasure fair.

The Battle of East Stoke

FOR nearly 100 years the families of the great Houses of York and Lancaster fought to secure their rival claims to the throne. The death of King Richard III, the head of the House of York, at Bosworth, Leicestershire, in 1485 and the accession of Henry VII, the head of the House of Lancaster, marked the date at which for England, medieval history ended and modern history began. However, the battle of East Stoke which was fought in Nottinghamshire two years later could be considered the last act of the Wars of the Roses.

The battle was the result of a Yorkist plot to unseat the new king, Henry VII, and restore the House of York by supplanting him with the young pretender, Lambert Simnel, who claimed to be Edward, Earl of Warwick, son of the murdered Duke of Clarence, and nephew of Edward IV and Richard III. The real Warwick had been imprisoned in the Tower of London where he was believed to have died.

Simnel, said to be the son of an Oxford joiner, was the pupil of a young priest named Richard Symonds, one of the architects of the plot, who believed that if successful Lambert would make him Archbishop of Canterbury. There was a great deal of Yorkist support in Ireland and

Lambert was shipped off to that country by Symonds and his conspirators. Simnel's claim was accepted by Edward IV's sister, Margaret Dowager Duchess of Burgundy and by other Yorkist sympathisers.

On the 24th May 1487, Simnel was crowned as Edward VI in Dublin Cathedral. New coins were struck, a Parliament was convened and plans made to invade and conquer England. The Duchess of Burgundy provided 2,000 German mercenaries for the cause, and a force of poorly armed Irish levies was raised in preparation for an English battle. The Earl of Lincoln was in charge of these forces and his second in command was a Nottinghamshire man, Francis, Lord Lovel.

On 4th June 1487 Lincoln's army landed in Lancashire and marched to York. Not receiving the help they had expected they turned south and came through Sherwood Forest, intent upon seizing Newark.

Henry had begun to muster his troops in the Midlands, around Kenilworth. When he heard news that his enemy had landed he immediately sent his men to Nottingham in order to prevent the enemy from crossing the Trent, thus stopping them marching towards the south. In Nottingham he was to receive 6,000 more troops.

The king's troops camped in Bunny Woods on 12th June and the next day his advance guards were at Nottingham. The main portion camped in a bean field some three miles from the town, some say at Holme Pierrepont and others plump for Clifton. The following night the royal army bivouacked in the meadows below Nottingham, beneath the Castle Rock and in the fields stretching towards Lenton.

It was Lincoln's intention that his army should cross the Trent close to Nottingham and on Friday 15th June he arrived at Fiskerton Ferry. It was probably easy to cross the river at that time of the year as the water would have been low. His troops camped on the high ground near to the villages of East Stoke and Elston. The king's troops were alerted and spent the night at Radcliffe-on-Trent.

Henry VII considered Saturdays to be his lucky day, and early on 16th June, his 'day of good fortune', he heard two masses by his chaplains. The trumpets sounded his men to arms and, accompanied by six good men of Radcliffe who showed him the way, his advance guard arrived by nine o'clock that morning at East Stoke.

This party met with Lincoln's main force, drawn up to stop their way between East Stoke and Elston. Historians believe that the Yorkist left wing was placed on the high ground between the Fosse and the village of Elston and their line ran westwards from there, across the highway and over Stoke fields to where the land dropped steeply down to the Trent valley.

Lincoln is thought to have attacked as soon as the king's forward column appeared, who bore the brunt of the struggle. The battle was 'stubborn, fierce and bloody'. After a great struggle in the open fields surrounding the two villages, Henry's men eventually gained the advantage. The remains of Lincoln's army tried to escape down the steep narrow track over Stoke Marshes which led to Fiskerton Ferry. Now they were an easy prey for the king's men, who slaughtered them in this gulley which is now known as 'Red Gutter', as it once flowed with the enemy's blood. This hollow, which is across the fields below Stoke Hall, is composed of red marl, hence its similarity with the colour of blood.

The enemy is estimated to have lost some 4,000 men, and the king's forces some 1,000 less in what was the bloodiest battle ever fought on Nottinghamshire soil.

The outcome confirmed the victory of Bosworth. Never again was the House of York to challenge the Tudor throne. This was the end of the terrible wars between rival families which had bedevilled the country for so long.

Symonds, the priest who had promoted Lambert Simnel,

was cast into a dungeon and no more was heard of him. Simnel's life was spared. He was taken prisoner on the field and later pardoned and made a scullion in the king's kitchen.

In addition to the 'Red Gutter', there is another reminder of the last of the Wars of the Roses. If you turn off the Fosse (now the A446) and head towards Elston, a few hundred yards down the road on the left hand side you will see a little spring, known by the locals as 'Willy Rungle'. It never freezes over, nor does it run dry. Elderly people will tell you how they always had a drink when they passed by in their younger days. Housewives used to draw water from the spring for domestic use.

However, the spring has a legend, for it is said that during the battle of East Stoke a dying soldier came to that point and was comforted by a villager. The soldier said, 'If I die and go to Paradise, a perennial spring will break forth in this place' and that was the origin of what much later was to become 'Willy Rungle'. Its clear water is a silent reminder of the death of some 7,000 men and the start of a new epoch.

Footpads and Highwaymen

TRAVELLING about the country in modern times can often be a frustrating experience, but spare a thought for the travellers of yesteryear who frequently had to contend with footpads and highwaymen.

Coaches bearing such wonderful names as the Nottingham Flying Machine and the True Briton were often under attack, as happened on 18th July 1764, when a coach was stopped by two highwaymen, who demanded money or the lives of its passengers. The guard whipped up his horses who shot off like greased lightning. The villains discharged their guns and the coach guard was badly wounded. He later died.

Many of these villains lurked in secluded places along the muddy cart-rucked ways and the better turnpike roads, waiting to relieve people of their goods and money. Indeed a highway robbery was almost to be expected when travelling any distance. Many people were reluctant to use the roads in the dark and delivering the mail was one of the most hazardous jobs after soldiering.

Looking through the Nottingham Date Book from 1750–1850, one is aware of the hazards of the high roads and byroads in the county. Horsedrawn conveyances were beyond the pockets of most folk, who had to walk long distances regardless of the weather. It was not unknown for people from Nottinghamshire to walk to London and back, all the time dreading robbers, and still more dreading the cost of food and lodging at public houses. Dick Turpin had been active in the county and people such as Thomas Wilcox, alias 'Sawley Tom', and George Brown, alias 'Bounds', had swung for their crimes.

Joseph Corden must have known of the risks as he was returning from Nottingham on 7th March 1827. He had nearly reached his home at six o'clock in the evening when a footpad crept from behind him and dealt him four cruel blows on the head. The victim described his ordeal to the court at his attacker's trial on 2nd April of that year.

He said that when he regained consciousness he remembered a man standing over him, ripping open his coat and waistcoat in search of valuables. This man continued to strike Corden who fought him as best he could. The assailant shouted, 'D--n your eyes, if you don't give me your money, I'll kill you!'

Fearing for his life the old man gave the robber all his money, which amounted to two sovereigns, a half-crown piece and some shillings and sixpences. He did not notice that his watch was missing until later.

As soon as his assailant was on the run, he told the court, he had shouted 'murder' and in less than half a minute a passerby called Grocock had captured the miscreant, a man called William Wells, and returned him to the scene of the assault.

Corden had then accused Wells of the crime, but the latter denied all knowledge, saying that the man he really wanted was last seen running up Basford Lane. Corden remained convinced that the right man had been standing in front of him at Basford and was now standing in front of him in the court.

John Grocock of Basford told the court that he was returning home and saw the prisoner robbing Mr Corden, whom he then heard crying, 'Oh dear, oh dear, I am robbed!' He saw Wells run up Basford Lane, caught him and enquired what he had been doing. Wells replied, 'Nothing.' Grocock in turn accused the man of attack and robbery, but was told the same story as that given to the victim — that the real thief was running up Basford Lane. Then the witness heard the prisoner throw something towards the hedge and a later search unearthed Mr Corden's watch, a small knife, a two-bladed penknife with one blade opened and a stout stick which was broken at one end. Wells was taken to the police that very night.

It did not take the jury long to pronounce Wells guilty as charged and the judge sentenced him to death, which was to take place on the following Tuesday.

William Wells was not a local man but had been born at Peterborough where he worked as a farm labourer. He had managed to save up a little money and started huckstering vegetables which he supplied to the barracks at Norman Cross near Peterborough, which housed the French prisoners of war.

He later married a respectable girl but took to gambling, which, as was the case with so many people, became his downfall. Then he set his sights on crooked horse-dealing and it is assumed it was around that time that he added spice to his life and money in his pocket through highway robbery.

During his trial Wells gave the appearance of being very cool and unflustered. Despite the terrible sentence dealt him on the Friday, he did not lose his appetite and ate heartily whilst he awaited his death. On the following Tuesday the execution was deferred, but no hopes of saving his life were expected. Wells became very contrite and took comfort from his spiritual instructors, not knowing if he were to die or be saved.

On the Saturday he was informed that his execution was fixed for the following Monday and again he received the information calmly. He counted the hours until the cart arrived to take him to the scaffold, where he was attended by three ministers who prayed with him for some time. Then he was placed upon the plank and joined the countless other criminals who had met their Maker from Gallows Hill, Nottingham. This terrible place was on the Mansfield Road, close to where the church cemetery now is. The footpad William Wells was the last person to be hanged there.

The Wrestling Baronet

THE village of Bunny was once famous for its annual wrestling match, which was established in 1712 by Sir Thomas Parkyns, Bart, of Bunny Hall.

Sir Thomas, who has been described as 'one of the most endearing eccentrics of the 18th century', was a man of diverse talents, being a lawyer, classical scholar, amateur architect, mathematician, squire and benefactor of Bunny and its neighbouring village Bradmore. He was the author of a book entitled *The Cornish Hug Wrestler* and designed and built many of the farmhouses in the district, some of which are still standing. In between all this he was a magistrate, and pointed out that the County Hall was in an unsafe condition. He was proved right during a crowded meeting in 1724 when the floor gave way and people fell through into the cellars.

Perhaps his most famous project was the wall he designed around Bunny Hall, which is built on a series of arches. He was also responsible for the design and erection of the school and almshouses at a personal cost of £400.

However, it was his love of wrestling which earned him the nickname 'The Wrestling Baronet'. At one time wrestling was a favourite sport in Nottinghamshire and like

today's cricket and football teams, there were inter-village matches which led to county contests.

From the start the Bunny event was extremely popular. The large, strong men would wrestle for the first prize of a gold-laced hat, value 22 shillings, and three shillings for the second best competitor. The wrestling was regulated by rules laid down by Sir Thomas who usually competed himself, along with his coachman and footman, who sometimes defeated him. The ring was permanent and during matches a chain was placed around its posted perimeter.

The park keeper used to take down the names of the competitors on separate slips of paper, and after shaking them up in a bag, he would draw two names out, who were immediately brought out to fight and the loser would have his ticket torn up. The winner's ticket was placed in another bag, for the next leg of the contest and so on until the match was won.

Sir Thomas died in 1741, aged 78 years. His penchant for wrestling is shown in his monument in Bunny church. It is divided in two sections. The one on the left contains the statue of the baronet in a wrestling attitude, and is said to bear a very strong resemblance to the life model, even to his wrestling cap and jacket which he wore when practising. Above the head of the statue is the motto 'Artificis status ipse fuit' which translates as 'This was the position of a wrestler'. In the lower part of the second right-hand section, the sporting baronet, still dressed as a wrestler, lies thrown at the feet of the Grim Reaper who is disguised as a cherub.

Like so many good things, it was the very appeal of the Bunny wrestling match which became its downfall. Over the years the event caused the 'idle and vicious of both sexes to congregate in multitudes, in a generally quiet village' and in 1811 it was stopped by Lord Rancliffe, the grandson of Sir Thomas. A man named Butler from Hucknall Torkard was the last winner of a prize.

The Shepherd's Race

THE maze known as the Shepherd's Race, or Robin Hood's Race, was cut on the top of a hill close to St Ann's Well and near to the chapel of St Ann at Sneinton Common. It was ploughed up after the Lordship of Sneinton was enclosed by an Act of Parliament in 1795.

These winding labyrinths were once a common feature throughout Britain. Many of the ecclesiastic ones were cut in the Middle Ages. For some curious reason mazes are enjoying a remarkable resurgence. There are now more than 100 in this country, compared with only about 40 a few years ago.

The Shepherd's Race is estimated to have had a diameter of 21 yards and the extreme distance between each projection was some 34 yards. Its winding path was about 536 yards long. Nobody can say for sure when it was built or by whom, but it was an unusual shape, being circular and with four horseshoe shapes forming a 'square' maze.

It is believed to have been cut out of the turf after the Roman period and certainly before the Reformation, after which period many rural mazes were converted into recreation attractions. Shakespeare refers to this in his *Midsummer Night's Dream*, Act II, Scene 2:

> 'The nine men's morris is fill'd up with mud;
> And the quaint mazes in the wanton green,
> For lack of tread are undistinguishable.'

The Shepherd's Race was lucky to have survived Cromwell's rule when many mazes and labyrinths were destroyed, being deemed to have pagan qualities. This Nottingham maze (and there was another square-shaped one at Clifton) was cut out of turf and it has been suggested that it could have had ecclesiastical origins. Maybe the monks at St Ann's chapel had it cut as a means of recreation, or perhaps it was a medium for performing penance for sins of omission and commission in general. This was quite a common function of mazes, the penitents being ordered to follow out all the winding pathways on their hands and knees, repeating so many prayers at fixed stations. Another theory is that it was cut by shepherds, hence its name.

However, the Shepherd's Race was well known for children and young lovers racing through its winding paths. Bradfield in *Pictures of the Past* (1864) gives a charming account of people amusing themselves at 'Sentan's Wells':

> 'Some run the "Shepherd's Race" — a rut
> Within a grass-plot deeply cut
> And wide enough to tread —
> A maze of path, of old designed
> To tire the feet, perplex the mind,
> Yet pleasure heart and head;
> 'Tis not unlike this life we spend,
> And where you start from, there you end.'

Sadly it was ploughed up on 27th February 1797. Later a facsimile was cut in the grounds of Poynters Tea Garden which stood on Blue Bell Hill, overlooking the valley of St Ann's Well and not far removed from the original 'Race'.

This authentic miniature was shaped by box hedging, and the paths were narrow and covered with Beeston gravel, which made running impossible. The Poynters had a half-clipped standard poodle which had been trained to run the maze for a penny. Being an untrustworthy dog he often took short cuts, yet always demanded payment from his onlookers. He would rush off to his mistress with his coin in his mouth, which he exchanged for a titbit. The Poynters' smart poodle was an added attraction to the tea garden.

However, the model could never have offered the same fun as the real thing, as described by the local historian, Blackner, in the 19th century, who lamented its destruction:

> 'A spot of earth, comprehending about 324 square yards (only about the 15th part of an acre) sanctified by the lapse of centuries as a place of rustic sport, by the curiosity of its shape and by the magic raptures which the sight of it awakened in our fancies of the existence of happier times, could not escape the hand of avarice which breaks down the fences of our comfort — the mounds of our felicity — and destroys the reverence of custom, if an object of gain or of ambition presents itself to view.
>
> 'Here the youth of Nottingham were wont to give felicity to the circulation of their blood; strength to their limbs, and elasticity to their joints, but callous-hearted avarice has robbed them of the spot.'

The Bramley Apple

WHAT'S in a name? Quite a lot, once it has been established. If Mr Herbert had made famous the usefulness of meat or other fillings placed between two pieces of bread before the fourth Earl of Sandwich, we would be eating cheese and pickle herberts! There would be no wellington boots, without the Duke of Wellington and no bowler hats without Mr Bowler the hat maker. What is more we would not be eating Bramley apples without Mrs Brailsford's son-in-law, Matthew Bramley.

It was in the 1820s that Mary Ann Brailsford planted a few apple pips in her cottage garden at Church Street, Easthorpe, Southwell, and quite by accident produced the first tree to bear these large shining green apples which have become one of the favourites of British cooks.

However it was her son-in-law, Mr Matthew Bramley, who inherited the cottage and lived to see the tree flourish and produce heavy crops of fruit which he gave to his friends and neighbours.

In 1856 Mr Henry Merryweather, the son of the founder of the Southwell Nursery, met someone carrying a basket full of this fine fruit. Being unable to identify the variety he asked where the apples came from and was told about Mr Bramley's superb tree. The nurseryman called at the cottage and was given permission to take grafts from the tree. It was from these grafts that Mr Merryweather produced the first of the Bramley seedling apples, named after Matthew Bramley, which soon became firm favourites for all forms of sweet and savoury cooking.

Mrs Brailsford's tree was planted in what is now 73 Church Street, and recently a parcel of land containing the tree was conveyed to the adjoining property, No 75. It is a good-shaped tree which continues to produce a fine crop each year and its cuttings remain viable. The tree attracts many visitors to this private garden.

Thanks to science the old tree has now been perpetuated by cloning, undertaken by the botany department of Nottingham University. In March 1990 the three ft cloned tree was planted by Sir Gordon Hobday, the Lord Lieutenant of Nottinghamshire at H. Merryweather and Sons' garden centre at Southwell. Cloning gives a much closer reproduction than can be achieved by growing from a seed or grafting.

The elderly tree has not only had to withstand age and the threat of disease. Its progeny has had to brace up to attack from the Common Market. Apparently decent-sized cooking apples are not grown in Europe as they need the wet and warm conditions of a typical English summer. The EEC categorized Bramleys as a 'low rate dessert apple'. Mr Henry Merryweather's great-grand daughter, Mrs Celia Stevens, was one of those who led the successful campaign to gain recognition for the Bramley apple in Europe.

Robin Hood

DID Robin Hood ever exist? Was he the Earl of Huntingdon, or merely a common outlaw. No matter what his origins, Robin Hood is inextricably connected with Nottinghamshire and with Sherwood Forest.

Some historians have suggested that this outlaw's supposed activities may have taken place in the reign of Henry III (1216–1272). It could be argued that if Robin Hood had existed there would have been some documentary evidence of his activities in the court records of that time, which is not the case. However, in later years his name became a popular alias for a number of criminals over a long time span. For outlaws did plague travellers through Sherwood Forest during the Middle Ages and use its secret places as their hideaway. They did hunt the king's deer, and the Sheriffs of Nottingham did terrorise the peasant farmers.

The little church at Edwinstone in the heart of Sherwood Forest is the reputed setting for the marriage between Robin and Marian, but as the latter character was not introduced into the tales until the 16th century this seems doubtful. Blidworth is the legendary birthplace of Robin's bride, which for the same reason has to remain suspect, and Will Scarlet, one of Robin's Merry Men is thought to be buried in Blidworth churchyard.

Locksley in Yorkshire and Hathersage in Derbyshire both claim to be the burial place of Robin Hood, the latter town also being the home of Little John, who was Robin's

second in command. The putative grave slab of this huge man now stands in the porch of the local church. In 1652 it was recorded that Little John's hat, bow, arrows and quiver were kept in the local church. They were removed in 1729 and the bow now resides in Scotland. Locksley is also the reputed birthplace of Robin.

The original tales of Robin and his Merry Men came from medieval ballads which were not sung but recited. These early sources were not documented and were consequently subject to variations and revision during their oral transmission. Onwards from that period some 38 ballads were composed.

One of the earliest manuscripts is entitled *Robyn Hod in Scherewod Stod* and Sherwood Forest has the closest associations with the man who robbed the rich to give to the poor. This is where the Major Oak still stands, its ancient branches propped and banded against age and decay. Seven hundred years ago the outlaws were said to have gathered under its sprightly form, dressed in their Lincoln green. It was in another large oak called Robin Hood's Larder that they hung their contraband venison. This tree has now succumbed to old age, as has the Parliament Oak or Trysting Tree under which Robin assembled his 'faithful commons'. Unfortunately, despite their romantic links, these three trees were not even saplings in the 13th century.

The longest and most famous tale, *A Gest of Robyn Hode*, is also thought to be the earliest written source, first published around 1510 although the spoken ballads date from before the 13th century. It was in the 16th century that Robin Hood sometimes replaced the May King and presided over the maypoles, Morris dancers and archery contests held at this festival which marked the first day of summer. The Robin Hood play formed part of the entertainment, which dealt with many of his adventures, and Maid Marian was first mentioned at that time. She took the place of Matilda fitz Walter, who in tradition from the

14th century had been the subject of the lecherous King John's attentions.

One of the first Robin Hood plays to be absorbed into the May games was that based upon the ballad *Robin Hood and the Curtal Friar*, being a friar who wore a short cloak. This tells the story of Friar Tuck and Robin's first meeting, which was on the bridge at Fountain Dale, Nottinghamshire, the village being the reputed birth and burial place of this military monk.

It was Joseph Ritson who made the first comprehensive set of ballads one century later and gave emphasis to Robin's anti-establishment activities. He wrote of this outlaw's life in Sherwood Forest: 'In these forests, and with this company, he for many years reigned like an independent sovereign; at perpetual war with the King of England and all his subjects, with the exception however of the poor and the needy, or such as were desolate and oppressed, or stood in need of his protection.'

In the 19th century Robin Hood became romanticised into our now accustomed hero when his adventures were absorbed into children's literature. Pierce Egan wrote *Robin Hood and Little John* in 1840 and many authors followed suit. The 20th century gave further emphasis to romance and adventure in literature and popular films starring such screen idols as the swashbuckling Errol Flynn and Richard Green.

Robin Hood has travelled a long way over almost 800 years. Never portrayed as a villainous highwayman or footpad, he evolved as a bright young blade, cleanly dressed in clothes of Lincoln green, the defender of the poor and justice. Robin never molested a hind at the plough or a thresher in his barn, neither did he take liberties with the fairer sex. He spent much time relieving maidens in distress, whilst widows and fatherless children looked to him for care. This outlaw was the champion of old women, the sick and disadvantaged. He became a May Day tradition, a romantic figure in print and then a silver screen heart throb. His exploits delighted audiences both in verse and song. Irrespective of the medium, Robin Hood must surely be one of the most famous and well loved of all our English folk heroes.

The Fools From Gotham

MANY people are familiar with the name Gotham (which in Nottinghamshire is pronounced as 'Got-ham'), from the nursery rhyme:

> 'Three wise men of Gotham
> Went to sea in a bowl;
> And if the bowl had been stronger,
> My song would have been longer.'

However, there are many more tales of fantasy connected with this village and it begins with the legend that when King John was making a trip to Nottingham Castle he had to pass through the village of Gotham. In those days it was believed that wherever the king walked it was from that day a royal highway, with public rights of way.

In order to prevent the loss of cattle grazing land the Gothamites conceived a cunning plan to dissuade the king from passing through their village. When the monarch's advance party came to their village they would feign lunacy and play at being harmless fools and this should be sufficient to keep the royal party away.

When the king's scouts came upon Gotham, to their amazement they found several of the villagers trying to drown an eel in a pond. Others were trying to put a fence around a cuckoo, saying that by trapping the bird it would be springtime all the year round. Cuckoo Bush Mound can still be found at Gotham. The king's men then saw some men tumbling cheeses down a hill, saying they were trying to roll them into Nottingham Market Place. Lunacy was abroad. The cunning plan worked, for the king circumnavigated Gotham and the grazing rights were retained.

Dr Andrew Borde, an eminent physician at the time of Henry VIII, is reputed to have written the first book about the fools (or wise men) of Gotham. This work is entitled *Certaine Merry Tales of the Mad Men of Gotham* and is said to be lodged in the Bodleian Library at Oxford.

There is the tale of a man who rode to market with two bushels of wheat, and to ensure that his horse did not have to carry the burden on its back, he carried it on his own and sat astride the horse.

Then there was the smith who had a wasps' nest in the thatch roof over his smithy. His customers complained of the wasps and so the smith got a red hot poker and shoved it in the middle of the nest. His thatch went up in flames and he replied proudly, 'I told thee I would fire them forth of their nest.'

A Gotham woman was given instructions by her husband to wet the meal before giving it to the pigs. She therefore threw the meal into the well and the pigs after it!

Another story tells of difficulties at a Gotham wedding. The priest who was marrying the happy couple said to the groom, 'Say after me.' The fool said 'After me.'

The priest said, 'Say not after me such words, but say after me, as I will tell thee.' The fellow said, 'Say not after me such words, but say after me, as I will tell thee.' After more of this the priest could not tell what to say, but said, 'What shall I do with this fool?' The fellow said, 'What shall I do with this fool?' 'Farewell,' said the priest. 'I will not marry thee.' 'Farewell,' said the fellow, 'I will not marry thee.' The priest departed but eventually the fool was married by a more tolerant man of God.

There are 20 tales in Borde's book, many of which have plots similar to those found in traditional pantomime. The stories have been reprinted many times and there are naturally several variations, but they all chart the harmless foolery of the people from Gotham.

Ned Ludd

THE early 19th century framework knitters of Nottinghamshire made stockings on machines which had been invented in the reign of Queen Elizabeth I. In 1589 William Lee, a native of Calverton, Nottinghamshire, devised the stocking-frame, which revolutionised the hosiery trade in the Midlands. A popular romantic story says this came about because he was fed up with the way in which his lover paid more attention to her knitting than to himself. Producing a machine for knitting silk stockings would mean she would have more time for courting.

Nine years later he presented a pair of silk stockings, made on his new, improved knitting frame, to Queen Elizabeth I in the hope that she would endorse the machine. However, neither she nor her successor, James I, encouraged Lee as they thought there would be too much trouble from redundant hand knitters. The inventor emigrated to France and set up his machines in Rouen, where he died in 1610.

His brother James returned to Nottinghamshire where he started a partnership with a mill owner using the machinery invented by brother William. In 1614 there were just two master hosiers making machine-knitted stockings in Nottingham, but by the end of that century the stocking trade was booming, with 60 per cent being made from silk.

Stockings were manufactured both in factories and by cottage workers operating their own frames. Therefore it was a trade conducted in both towns and villages. Some outworkers managed to buy their machines, others were the property of merchants who rented them out at a weekly rent. Other people rented weekly space in a 'shop of frames' containing eight or ten frames. However, although some worked all hours of the day and most of the night, it was becoming harder to earn a decent living.

In 1778 the framework knitters applied to Parliament to raise the rate of wages, to lower the charge for frame-rent and to prevent abuses and frauds in the trade. They were an independent class of men, proud of their craft and determined to claim their rights as they saw them. Their petition was presented by Daniel Parker Coke, MP for Derby. It stated that they had served regular apprenticeships and had always employed themselves in making stockings, mitts and gloves on the stocking-frame, of silk, cotton, thread and worsted, but despite their hard work they were incapable of providing the basic necessities of life for their families. This was not only on account of their small wages, but the paying of frame-rent and other costs needed to keep the machines in working order.

The merchant-hosiers, who had formed themselves into an association, appointed Mr Samuel Turner, an attorney, as their agent and secretary. However, in fear of retribution from their workers, the hosiers did not speak out against them. Finding it necessary to produce some kind of defence against the petition, Turner induced two master stocking-makers, Henry Cox and James Thorpe, to give evidence, doubtless hoping this would persuade the hosiers to give them some backing.

The committee of the House, aware of the position of the hosiers, dispensed with the counter evidence, and made a report upon which the bill was founded. On 25th February the House voted 27 for its admission and 52 against.

The defeated petitioners were furious and poured their wrath upon Cox, Thorpe and 'Lawyer Turner'. Cox had his windows smashed, his family terrified and his life threatened. The other two had stones thrown through their bedroom windows whilst they were sleeping. The hosiers put up a reward of ten guineas for the discovery of the offenders. They were never found.

For the rest of that year the frameworkers acquired more followers, and large subscriptions were raised. A further petition was presented to Parliament in 1779. A committee was again appointed to enquire into its merits. The evidence attested the low rates of wages, and the high rate of frame-rent. A master stocking-maker proved that his workmen's clear earnings did not average seven shillings per week.

On behalf of the hosiers, Mr Need, a wealthy factory owner, in partnership with Richard Arkwright, the inventor of the spinning frame, stated in evidence that the workmen were sufficiently remunerated. Such were the advantages of the manufacture, they said, the more children a workman had, the better was his condition of life. A reduction in frame-rent would prove ruinous to the manufacture, by discouraging people from buying their frames. Furthermore, they threatened, if a bill was passed to restrict their business, the hosiers would sell their frames and retire from the trade as they should be undersold by the French.

They also produced evidence from a lad named Wilkinson, which lent great weight to their evidence. This youth, who was henceforth called 'the miraculous boy', swore that he could earn 20 shillings a week with great ease.

In May, leave to carry the bill was granted with just one dissenter. One MP speaking in its favour spoke as one 'moistened and saturated with the tears of the poor and their distressed families.' The Nottinghamshire workers were elated and throughout the county subscription lists were opened to raise money to carry the bill through its future stages. Tradesmen canvassed their customers, most public houses had their own list and almost every street and village had its own collector. The second reading, a short time after, was carried by a majority of one — 24 against 23, but on the third reading it was lost by a majority of 57 to 18.

News of the defeat reached Nottingham on 10th June, which coincided with a great holiday among the Jacobites, who wore white roses in honour of the Pretender's birthday.

In a very short time the town was in a ferment. The frameworkers rallied in the market place and at ten o'clock at night their anger burst into violence. They rushed into Parliament Street where they broke every pane of glass in the house of Mr James, a large hosiery manufacturer.

Then they proceeded to deliver the same treatment to other wealthy manufacturers, including the hated Mr Need, who with Richard Arkwright had spoken in favour of the hosiers earlier that year. Mr Wilkinson, who had produced 'the miraculous boy', had his windows broken and furniture smashed.

The magistrates had not anticipated any violence and they, in the company of the officers of the Royal Horse Guards, were attending a ball at the race stand. Upon the bugle sounding to arms at midnight, the officers mounted and rode into the market place dressed in their 'ball dresses' where they remained until daybreak.

The exasperated people resumed their work the following day, the magistrates read the Riot Act, and the crowd dispersed, to do its work elsewhere. Messrs Need and Arkwright's mills had their windows broken, the soldiers arrived too late and the men managed to smash up the home of 'Lawyer Turner' with ease.

The soldiers formed themselves into patrols to thwart the rioters, but eventually returned wearily to their quarters. No sooner had they dismounted and were feeding their horses than the house of a hosier called Churchill, who lived at Wheeler Gate, became the centre of an attack so violent that he thought it better to leave town rather than try to repair it.

Later that day the men tried to fire Need's mill, but the

soldiers were waiting for them. The frameworkers decided to leave some men at the mill, to engage the soldiers' attention, whilst others made a quick march of four miles to Arnold where they attacked Mr Need's country house, broke up his furniture, smashed up his staircase and brought the roof down. Whilst this was going on at Arnold, another mob broke into his town coach house where they destroyed his carriage and harness.

'Mr Need having been sufficiently punished,' says the *Nottingham Journal*, 'they all ran away, to sleep easy and happy.'

The next day saw similar disturbances but the next, being the Sabbath, was quiet. The following Monday the stockingmakers from the villages poured into Nottingham and enlarged mobs became even more violent. Frames were taken out and smashed in public, the shops of hosiers and middle men were violated. The town was in a feverish state. The Riot Act was again read, all business suspended and shops closed.

A report of the events states, 'In the height of the storm, oil was poured upon the troubled waters in a way which shows how powerfully an appeal to reason will sometimes triumph over the passions of a mob. About eight in the evening, an individual harangued the multitude, in the Market Place, and after exhorting them to behave more like citizens, assured them that the hosiers would hold a three counties meeting on the morrow, with a view to redress their grievances. Tranquillity was at once restored, two men who had been taken prisoner by the soldiers were released, the people went peacefully to their homes, and the soldiers to their quarters, as though nothing had happened.'

Unfortunately on 21st June the hosiers failed to meet the frameworkers' demands and violence resumed. The next day 300 of Mr Need's machines were destroyed at Arnold and Wilkinson's house was burned down.

The mayor issued a proclamation in which he stated that

'Further lenity would be a crime, and that the vigilance of justice should be exerted in its utmost severity.' The hosiers advertised that they were now one compact body, which would punish offenders and encourage those who were peaceably inclined. They later issued a further conciliatory advertisement, in which they stated they 'would remove every oppression, providing a cessation of the riot took place.' Rioting died down and the participants received their judicial punishment.

Over the years outbreaks of dissension continued on an ad hoc basis, but by 1811 it was clear that the outbreaks were becoming more organised and deliberate. The participants were no longer shouting mobs but trained gangs led by masked men following almost military principles. The name of the mythical 'General Ludd', or 'Ned Ludd' was signed on the bottom of inflammatory posters and handbills.

It is said that a Ned Ludd did actually exist. He was a simpleton with a ready temper who lived in a Nottinghamshire village and was tormented by the jibes of the local children. One day at the turn of the 19th century he chased a small boy who had been teasing him but the boy managed to escape. Ludd was so cross that he smashed up two knitting frames to vent his anger. Thereafter Ned was blamed for all the machinery destroyed in his area and became a useful scapegoat who quickly turned into a legend.

The first official Luddite violence is said to have been mustered by the Nottinghamshire frameworkers and took place in Nottingham Market Place on 11th March 1811, which led to the destruction of 60 frames.

Luddism quickly spread to many industrialised parts of England where the poverty stricken workers went 'Ludding'.

The name 'Ned Ludd' became synonymous with that of the bogeyman in many comfortable households. Their children were threatened with a visit from Ludd as an ultimate form of punishment. It was said that men who disregarded an order from 'General Ludd' risked death. The children from poor families were taught to hold him in great respect. Many followers of Ludd were imprisoned and executed but it did not deter their campaign to wage war on the bad conditions and poor wages which were the lot of the stockingmakers and cloth workers.

The 'Followers of Ned Ludd' continued their work in Nottinghamshire through to 1816, when the last reported incident was on 2nd November at Bulwell.

The final Luddite attack appears to have been in Leicestershire in 1817 when a large factory at Loughborough was attacked by a group of men armed with blunderbusses. Afterwards the last of the Luddite heroes was executed. The world had changed and the machine had come to stay.

Twist Fever

BEFORE the invention of the bobbin net machine, most lace in this country had been handmade on little pillows and known as Brussels point or 'pillow lace'. This was a time consuming and intricate task using a pattern pricked out by pins on parchment which was secured to the pillow or cushion. The thread was twisted into pattern by using bone bobbins, identified by coloured beads threaded into a circle through their head. Many of these bobbins bear messages of love or the owner's names, pricked out and coloured along the shaft — 'Love Come A Gain', 'Mary', 'Sarah'. They all bear a memory and are now highly collectable.

In 1809, Mr John Heathcote of Loughborough obtained letters patent for 14 years' protection of his invention of the bobbin net machine. During this period he and his partner, Mr Charles Lacey, levied a heavy tax upon copies of this machine. When the patent expired in March 1823, 'Speculation the most extensive and ruinous set in, and capitalists of every grade anxiously embarked their money in the bobbin net vortex.' The producers of the material manufactured on the new machines could turn out quantities of the stuff at a high retail price. It is said that soon after Heathcote's invention lace was sold at five guineas per yard. Twenty years later it was making 18 pence a yard. In the early days the machines gave their investors a tremendous return on their capital outlay.

Besides the usual business entrepreneurs, butchers,

bakers, bankers, clergymen, farmers, publicans, lawyers, in fact any one with a little money to spare or the power to borrow, invested in the lace bobbin machine which was to turn Nottinghamshire into the premier lace making county in England. Many people from outside the area became 'Lace Adventurers'. The lace manufacturers themselves appear to have owned no more than one third of the total number of machines.

The lace industry was not confined to Nottingham, but factories were also established in outlying areas such as Basford, Arnold, Beeston and Lenton. Cottage workers operated from their homes in the villages surrounding these towns.

Hundreds of mechanics, tempted by better wages, poured in from Sheffield, Birmingham, Manchester and other places. Money circulated freely and much of Nottinghamshire rode high on gain. People were in the first throes of 'Twist Fever'.

While the fever lasted the machine makers had the greatest share in the prosperity. Many could not meet the demand for their goods. The setters-up were the best paid workers. Their charge for adjusting a six quarter levers machine was £20 2s and took from two to three weeks to complete.

During the excitement the number of master smiths in the town and neighbourhood was more than trebled. Stables, kitchens, cellars and the most unlikely places were converted into smiths' or bobbin and carriage makers' shops.

With so many people flocking into the area to work in this 'golden industry', new houses were thrown up at an alarming rate. Rows and rows of back to back housing were crammed into Nottingham by greedy speculators who cared not a jot for the inhabitants' health or convenience. The price of land and materials rose. No sooner was a row of dwellings roofed and glazed than the chimneys were smoking and the rentals commenced.

It is said that the general enquiry was not so much, 'What is the rent?' as 'Will you let me a house?' In one instance a butcher who had been exhibiting a 'wonderful pig' in a common showman's caravan, 'ousted the porkine tenant, and stationing the vehicle in his garden at the back of York Street, actually let it to families as a dwelling place for two shillings and three pence a week.'

By 1825 the demand for lace had peaked and prices were falling, thus lowering the temperature of 'Twist Fever'. The more circumspect of the machine holders began to curtail their operations and gradually sold out. Some of these men had risen from nothing and by retiring in time made considerable fortunes. The majority, however, did not foresee the end of the initial boom and lost much of their investment.

By 1830 many of the Nottinghamshire lace workers had emigrated to France, where wages were rumoured to be some 60 per cent higher than in their home country.

As the market levelled out, so did the wages and conditions of work. Young children over the age of five years worked for perhaps 17 hours a day winding the thread onto machines. They slept on heaps of material thrown into the corners of their place of work. Some children were even kidnapped from the big cities and forced to work in the Nottinghamshire factories. The poor little mites were brought up in an environment of drink and worse and died an early and unnoticed death.

Many women 'lace runners' or embroiderers who worked from their humble homes did so for a mere pittance. Seated at their rented frames for long hours they handfilled with a needle and thread the lace patterns stamped on the plain net, earning about one halfpenny an hour. Others worked for females who rented work houses for their operatives and deducted fees from each woman for the use of the frame room. It was common for the ten women labouring in one room to cook a hash or stew in a corner for a few pence to feed themselves during their stay of up to 17 hours a day.

The women who attended the material after the lace runners' labours were better paid, but their task was even more ruinous to their eyesight. These 'lace menders' had to examine each piece of work and mend, with needle and thread, every defective mesh in the net. They were so skilled that their mending was quite invisible.

A commissioners' report was made on the housing and moral conditions of Nottingham in 1845. The streets of this rapidly filling town were 'generally narrow, unpaved, uneven, ill ventilated, noisome and damp, owing to the absence of sewerage. . . .' The houses 'have no back yards and the privies are in common to the whole court: altogether they present scenes of a deplorable character and of surprising filth and discomfort. The younger members of families are driven into the streets; and thus girls and youths, destitute of adequate house-room, and freed from parental control become accustomed to gross immoralities.'

Over the years the fortunes of the lace industry dipped and then soared to new heights so that by 1890 there were over 500 lace factories in Nottingham alone, employing some 17,000 people. It is said that some 80 yards of lace trimming were needed to complete a large Victorian skirt! In 1911 half the country's lace workers were working in Nottingham.

The high storeyed warehouse buildings which form part of the area in Nottingham known as the Lace Market were built to impress the buyers. This was also where the 'travellers' or lace representatives packed up their huge quantities of samples — sometimes more than 2,000 — and took them to all parts of the world. Only the finishing touches were done in these buildings, the actual production taking place elsewhere.

The industry's decline came from 1920–1926 when lace

lost its fashion appeal and the home market could not compete with cheaper foreign imports. During this period half the companies went bankrupt, but happily the lace industry still plays its part in the economy of Nottinghamshire today.

The Gypsy and The Lady

A LONG time ago a handsome young gypsy was walking towards Nottingham. When he drew close to the city he saw some large notices and stopped to read them. To his amazement they were advertisements announcing that a young, rich and beautiful widow who loved all that was good and charitable was in need of a well built husband.

Upon reaching the nearest tavern the newcomer asked around for the identity of this lonely but interesting woman. The gypsy was told that she really was a beautiful, rich young widow, who alas had not had much luck with her seven husbands. It was rumoured that these well built chaps all died off like flies after the honeymoon. Nobody could recollect any church burials, but they had probably gone into the family vault.

Yes, she owned a beautiful house, lovely furniture and had a different servant for each day of the week. All she was lacking at the moment was a strong, able bodied young husband. The Nottingham lads looked at the stranger and agreed amongst themselves that he was probably just the fellow she was seeking. They complimented him upon his height and generous yet muscular body. His thick shining hair was just waiting for the caresses of a fine lady! Never had they seen better brown eyes or white teeth in such a handsome face! Look at those muscles — he was as strong as a cart horse and as good as married to her already! Could he read? Of course he could or else he would not have known about Lady X! They wrote her address on a piece of paper and pushed it into his pocket, bidding him good luck and to remember them when he had pockets filled with gold.

Now the gypsy was poor and in need of a roof over his head. He was tired of wandering about from town to town doing odd jobs and being treated worse than a dog. A rich, good looking widow was just what he needed, but the thought of her seven dead husbands struck a warning note. However, he was made from healthy country stock and could well look after himself and keep the rich woman happy.

The next morning he bathed himself, straightened his clothes, spat on his boots, flexed his muscles and knocked on the door of the grand house. He was received by a maid who took one look at him and enquired if he had come to discuss matters of a delicate nature with her mistress?

He dismissed the boldness of her question, affirmed that he was indeed calling on matters of a personal nature and was duly presented to the widow, who surpassed his wildest dreams. Notwithstanding her fortune she was everything a young man could desire. Her refined beauty and gentle bearing quickly dispersed any doubts concerning her need to advertise for a husband. The rustic stood dumbfounded, gazing at her in anticipation.

The lady smiled at the gypsy boy, looked him up and down with the eye of one who knows what she is looking for, and without more ado announced that he would do very nicely. She suggested, rather vigorously even for a seasoned bride, that they should dispense with a long engagement for she had been without a husband for long enough. In her eyes, she confided, he was absolutely delicious!

A grand wedding was arranged in as short a space as it takes to organise such a splendid event. The couple were married and the now familiar ceremony was tolerated by her friends and relations, who were intrigued by her choice of eighth husband. After the nuptials there was much roistering and eventually it was time for the newly-weds to retire to their chamber.

All went well until the young man awoke in the night and found his bride was missing. He called out for her, but she did not respond. He hunted all over the great mansion for his beloved, but she was nowhere to be found.

Being used to sleeping rough he was not versed in the ways of the rich. He dismissed the absent bride as being a common custom amongst the gentrified people of Nottinghamshire and so retired to bed and was soon fast asleep. The following morning, his bride was snuggled up close beside him, enquiring if he had slept well. He did not like to say that he had found her missing so he smiled contentedly and said that he had slept like any happy bridegroom.

'My love,' crooned the bride, 'you are so beautiful I could devour you, my big dimpled duckling!'

The same thing happened the next night although she was back beside him in the morning, again enquiring in an adoring manner if he had had an uninterrupted sleep. He replied that his sleep was as sound as that of the dead.

'Sweet gypsy boy,' she whispered, 'I hunger for you!'

On the third night the new husband only pretended to be sleeping and felt his wife slip gently out of bed in her usual manner. With half closed eyes he watched her dress silently and skilfully in the full moonlight. Then she tiptoed across the room, carefully opened the door and was away like a shot.

He followed her at a safe distance, out through the house, into the garden and along a narrow pathway which led to a remote part of the grounds which he had not visited before. The moon was so bright he could see clearly from a safe distance as she approached what looked like mounds. He moved a few steps forward and counted them, one, two, three, four, five, six, seven.

The woman knelt down and started to dig at one of them with her bare hands. He edged a little closer and saw her burrowing as furiously and excitedly as a terrier at a foxhole. The gypsy crept closer still, with all the skills of a master poacher and the cunning of his ancestors, yet his heart was banging like a tin drum.

When he was just a few terrible feet away from his darling wife she stopped clawing at the ground and started to tear at something with her teeth. She let out loud grunts of satisfaction as she pushed more delicacies into her now decidedly unladylike mouth. A few more silent moves and he was able to see that she was gorging herself on meat which smelled far worse than an old paunched rabbit.

She reached in for lumps of the stuff which she swallowed like a beast, occasionally freeing her lips of spittle and earth which she wiped on her silken sleeve. She snarled and drooled over the tough bits and swallowed the tender pieces whole. She was totally happy as she guzzled and belched her way through that atrocious midnight feast.

The bridegroom could stand the sight no longer. He broke cover and pulling himself to his full height demanded to know what she was eating. The bride looked round, stood up and faced him with no hint of shame on her once lovely face, which was now filled with hatred and evil. She grinned nastily as she flung a rock at his skull and screamed out 'I'm eating corpse, you fool, I'm eating husband corpse!'

Old Sherwood Forest

OLD Sherwood Forest was once much larger than it is today. In 1300 it was roughly 20 miles in length by eight wide. At one extremity was Nottingham, at another Mansfield, whilst Worksop was close to the northern boundary. The forest contained some 100,000 acres, or nearly one fifth of the county.

During the winter of 1222 a terrible storm is said to have swept over England. Trees were overthrown in such huge numbers that special writs were quickly issued prohibiting the Sherwood Forest administrators from claiming their perquisites of fallen boughs or root-fallen trees. Instead the overthrown timber had to be sold and was accountable in the forest returns.

Some interesting forest offences came to light when the Forest Pleas or Eyres, presided over by the king's justices, were held at Nottingham. These courts were supposed to be held every seven years but in reality were held at much longer and fitful intervals. The earliest recorded court was held in 1251, when the forest was divided into three keepings or wards, each of which had their own verderers, foresters and agisters. The latter regulated the pasturage and the pannage of pigs permitted within that area.

At the Eyre of 1267, several hundred vert offences were brought before the court for damage to the growing timber. The most serious was that of the Abbot of Rufford, who was charged with felling 483 oaks for building material since the last session. However, he successfully mitigated his offences by pleading a charter of Henry II.

It appears that the next Forest Court was not summoned until 1286. During the preceding year there had been a catastrophic outbreak of murrain amongst the deer, both red and fallow, from which 350 had perished.

Special injunctions regarding future administration were laid down on this occasion. It was agreed that any dweller in the forest caught felling a tree was to be summonsed to the next Attachment Court, there to find bail until the next Eyre, and to pay the fine to the verderers. For a second offence he was to be dealt with in the same manner, but for a third offence he was to be placed in Nottingham gaol, 'and there to be kept until delivered by the king or justice of the forest.'

Anyone living outside the forest caught cutting any greenwood was to be placed in prison and dealt with as above for his first two offences. For a third he was also to forfeit his horses and cart, or his oxen and waggon.

It was also laid down that the verderers were to assemble every 40 days, to hold Attachment Courts for vert, venison and other small pleas. Also known as the Forty-Day Court, or the 'Swaynmote', these were held on a regular basis over a very long period and were held at Calverton, Edwinstowe, Linby and Mansfield on successive days of the week.

In 1316 the Archbishop of York's great wood at Blidworth was being administered by the king, as the see was vacant. Edward II ordered the forest keeper to deliver to the sheriff 50 leafless oaks out of that wood, to be used for making charcoal and for boards and trestle tables. Likewise 30 oaks from parts of the forest near the Trent were to be sent to Nottingham Castle for firewood in the king's hall and 30 more for the king's chambers.

Even in woods in private ownership within royal forests, there was no power of felling timber or cutting wood, except for immediate personal use, without a direct royal warrant.

An interesting use of timber was entered in the Close Rolls towards the end of 1323–24 when an expedition was about to be undertaken into the Duchy of Aquitaine. The Sheriff of Nottingham and his carpenters were instructed to procure as many oaks and other suitable trees out of the forest, as were necessary for the construction of nine springalds and a thousand quarrels. The former were military catapults and the latter arrows with iron heads which these catapults discharged.

The general custom which prevailed in most of England's royal forests concerning their tenants was for them to have the use of wood for the repair or building of their houses, for the construction of hedges and for the purposes of fuel. This was viable throughout Sherwood.

The largest and most substantial beams used in the construction of St Paul's Cathedral were provided by the grand oaks of Sherwood Forest. Papers held at Welbeck Abbey are said to include a letter from the architect, Sir Christopher Wren, dated 4th April 1695, addressed to the steward of the Duke of Newcastle. He states the required dimensions of the 'great Beames' which were to be '47 ft long, 13 inches at the small end, of growing timber, and as near as can be without sap.'

In 1531 Henry VIII appointed a commission to view and certify the number of deer in the forest and parks of Sherwood. The red deer numbered 4,280 and the fallow 1,131. The former ranged through the forest, and 200 were contained in Bestwood Park. The fallow deer were within the four parks of Bestwood, Clipstone, Nottingham and Thorney.

Queen Elizabeth, in 1599, granted the keepership of the forest district of Thorneywood, to the north of Nottingham, to John Stanhope, with licence to hunt, chase and kill the deer, provided he always found a hundred head for the use of the queen. During the Commonwealth a large number of deer vanished from the forest and in 1661 Charles II had to find a considerable sum of money to import red and fallow deer from Germany for the restocking of both Sherwood and Windsor Forests.

The monarch did his best to revive the forest laws of Sherwood in 1662. The business placed before the new Forest Court was so complicated that although it opened at Mansfield in February 1663 the proceedings were not concluded until 1676. Claims to special privileges were put forward by numerous people including the Archbishop of York, Sir George Savile of Rufford, Lord Byron of Newstead and others who had succeeded to monastic properties sacked by Henry VIII. Scores of minor claimants came from all parts of the forest and its surroundings, pleading privileges which existed in the old days to particular towns and parishes.

In 1708 a strongly worded petition was drawn up at Rufford by representatives of the north of the county, addressed to the Crown. They complained of the almost intolerable burden placed upon landowners by the increasing number of red deer in Sherwood Forest. So many of the woods had been granted or given away by Queen Anne's predecessors there was little shelter for the deer, who were scattered all over the county eating up grass and corn. During times of severe weather their tenants had to sit up all night to scare the beasts away. Their tenants were being terrified by newly appointed keepers who threatened them if they so much as set a little dog on the intruding animals. However, the petition received short shrift as it was argued that to attempt to cut down the number of deer through Parliament would be detracting from the queen's liberties and rights.

Reports presented to the Commissioners of Woods and Forests in 1793 showed that there were then no deer in the forest save in Thorney Woods, of which Lord Chesterfield was keeper. A great many deer were to be found in Birkland and Bilhagh until about 1770, when they were killed off, with the assistance of the local people, by the Dukes of Newcastle and Kingston. In a short time the value of the forest farms increased and the wheat fields no longer needed to be guarded by horns in the daytime and by fires at night.

The forest has changed beyond imagination since its legendary days of Robin Hood. It now shelters an all weather holiday village and tourist centre instead of old style outlaws and bandits. Yet notwithstanding commercial interests, there are still many beautiful places to explore far removed from the crowds.

Cries of Old Nottingham

THERE are still a few street vendors shouting their wares in the centre of Nottingham, but this is literally a far cry from the days still within memory, when the air was busy with their calls. The surrounding villages and towns also had their share of shouting. Shopping was certainly a different experience in the days of 'Juicy Yemons' and 'Professor' Brown, the 'Swell Quack Doctor'!

Many older readers will probably remember the man shouting 'Coal-e-oh! coal-e-oh!' and people going out to buy their coal which was weighed on large scales from the back of his cart, the gentle horse waiting patiently with its velvet nose stuck in its nosebag.

Then there was the scissors, saws and knives grinder, who walked for miles pushing his cart with its big treadle wheel which drove the smaller grinding wheel.

In the days before mass communication it was common for the *Nottingham Journal* and the *Nottingham Evening News* to print special 'Stop Press' editions, almost hourly, to keep people abreast of important news or some terrible disaster. Well into the night an army of chaps would run around the streets of Nottingham and its neighbouring areas calling, 'Read all about it, read all about it! Such-and-such disaster, read all about it!' and they always had plenty of buyers.

The Rag and Bone Man was always a favourite with children who eagerly awaited his call, 'Rags a' bones, bottles

MUSHY
PEAS
1d
FLY
PAPERS

a' jumpers!' as he walked up their street, pushing his cart. He would give them a little gaily coloured paper windmill attached to a stick in return for a few items. If there was a lot of stuff to get rid of then 'mother and father took it out and got a copper.' After the 1930s the children's reward was upgraded to a goldfish which soon died from lack of proper care.

Rabbits were a cheap form of meat, and 'rabbit men' were everywhere, calling out to housewives, 'Do you want to buy a rabbit? I'll sell you one for sixpence. Do you want it skinning? I'll sell you one for a bob!' Then a suitable animal would be selected from his handcart and it was rabbit stew for dinner.

One old man called out 'Buy a-rabbit, cheap a-rabbit' over and over as he stood in the centre of Nottingham with one armful of skinned rabbits and the other armful of unskinned ones.

'Buy a-rabbit, cheap a-rabbit' mingled with 'Now you fish buyers. . . .' This was the cry in the Market Place emanating from the fish stalls, where sometimes on hot Saturday nights the fish spoke for itself. There was old Hack Rowe calling 'Mussels-alive-O!' at the top of his shrill voice and another man in a top hat announcing 'Fine new shrimps, fresh come in!' These calls intermingled with 'Fine oily kippers!' and 'Pyclets!'

One strange man used to walk around the city wearing a top hat decorated with fly papers on which were stuck hundreds of captive insects. He invited people to catch flies his way: 'Catch em' alive, O! All alive!' Little boys were happy when their mothers bought fly papers, which were hung from the ceiling and dripped sweet glue onto the floor on hot days. Not only did the long papers get caught up in unwary adults' hair, they provided hours of fun for certain children who enjoyed watching the winged insects buzzing themselves to eventual death. Sweets and marbles have been known to change hands when making bets on which would die first.

Nothing was more welcome on a cold winter's night than to hear the Hot Pea Man calling 'Hot peas, smoking hot!' A penny would buy a big dollop of mushy peas which came from the old pea can which the trader carried on his arm. Whenever the river Trent was sufficiently frozen for skating, there he was, with his little portable stove, standing on the ice calling 'Hot peas, smoking hot!' with queues of nipped fingers clutching their pennies, anxious for a lovely hot feast in the open air.

His greatest rival must have been the 'penny hot pie man' who carried his pies in a tin which he slung across his back. He too had a makeshift stove on four legs where he kept his pies 'all nice and hot'.

A regular cry on the eastern side of the city came from an old sailor who called out 'Onion nets, a penny each! It's a charity to buy one from a poo-or old sailor!' It was indeed a hard heart who could refuse such a pitiful, and possibly rich, old man.

'Now for yer blue-buttons!' This was not the message of a tailor but another 'old salt' offering mushrooms for sale.

Again within memory there was a very old chimney sweep who used to waken sleeping people at an ungodly hour of the morning by crying out in a voice which belied his age, 'Do yer want yer chimney sweepin?'

Apparently most of the Nottingham chimney sweeps saved their soot for the annual football match which took place between the Sweeps v the Bakers, which used to be played, or rather fought, for the benefit of the hospital. This match was always accompanied by a flour and soot flinging contest.

'Cane chairs to bottom and mend' boomed the chair mender as he walked around the city, carrying an armful of canes and a kneeling mat. He would call out his first two words loudly and let the second word 'swell' and then quicken up his beat on the last four.

The old man who once stood in the Market Place wearing a peaked cap bearing the message 'God is Love' has long since cried his last invitation to 'Corn salve, a penny a packet!' He was a tall, bent man, who pushed a home made barrow constructed from a soapbox on pram wheels. After making his first announcement he would call out in a softer voice to the women, 'Now then you gels, who've got corns and wants to meet yer sweethearts, here's corn salve, a penny a packet!'

'Coughdrops, a penny a packet!' was barked by a hoarse throated vendor with a big black tin trunk full of cough drops which stood beside him in the market place. This man sported a moustache which was as large and bushy as a yard brush. 'Old Wolfy', as the boys called him, was always to be seen at the Nottingham football matches, selling his wares, dressed in a shabby suit and an old bowler hat.

A man called 'Juicy Yemons' was good bait for the teasing of the local Nottingham lads. This unfortunate hawker of lemons who usually stood outside the Mechanics' Hall 'talked half short-tongued and half something else'. He was quick tempered and if anyone dared to look at his basket without buying one of his 'yemons' he soon told that person where to go.

Another well known Nottingham character was 'Tommy Tittlemouse' who sold 'racing certainties', gained from information straight from the 'orses' mouth, at a great financial outlay to himself.

One puzzling cry was that of a fruit hawker who used to shout:

> 'Apples a pound pears,
> Plums the same!'

He took his fruit round on a handcart which he pushed down the middle of the street. Then he would stop and shout again his strange nonsense call.

It would be foolish to think that all these folk went about selling and shouting in sweet harmony. Disturbances did break out between the street hawkers. On one unforgettable occasion, 'Professor' Brown the 'Swell Quack Doctor' came to grief with a 'Model Nottingham Auctioneer' when they had a massive quarrel in front of a large crowd of people. The Nottingham *Owl* of 14th May 1886 reported that the 'Knight of the Hammer' had called the 'Learned Professor' an ignorant quack and said all his medications were worthless. He then went on to malign the quack's lady friend who gave lectures from his gilded chariot. The 'Model Auctioneer' in turn was accused of being a scoundrel and an ignoramus of the deepest dye.

Most of the lively old characters had gone by the late 1920s or early 1930s; all the men and women who had scraped some sort of living from calling their wares and mending and selling myriads of things which kept a house and its inhabitants ticking over. The more outrageous the character, the better the chance of a sale. These hawkers and opportunists throbbed with the city and shuffled into its outreaches with colourful determination. Quack doctors produced 'miracle cures', Punch and Judy shows performed in the streets and until the end of the 19th century, even bears danced in Nottingham.

Pins and Kitty Hudson

KITTY Hudson was born at Arnold in 1765 but at the age of six years she went to live with her grandfather at Nottingham. He was the sexton of St Mary's church and arranged for Kitty to clean the building as a contribution towards her board and lodging. It was within the hallowed walls of the mother church of Nottingham that the child's addiction was formed.

If Kitty found a pin whilst sweeping the floor she popped it into her mouth and gave it to her grandfather's housemaid upon her return home. This greatly amused the servant who egged the child on to do the same the next day.

'Kitty,' she would say, 'If you'll get me a mouthful of pins I'll give you a stick of tuffy!'

The little girl loved her toffee and quickly grew to rely upon the sensation of pins in her mouth. Soon life became unbearable without them. She could neither eat without several stuck into her mouth, nor could she sleep without them. Kitty Hudson was addicted to pins.

Time passed, her back teeth were almost worn down to the gums through grinding on pins but pain in her mouth no longer satisfied her craving. She turned her body into an agonising but secret pincushion with limbs numbed and swollen from her cruel attentions. Eventually her right arm became so painful she had to be admitted to the infirmary.

Upon examination two pins were extracted from deep in the flesh above the wrist and many more were pulled from that hideously swollen and pulsating arm. However this did not stop the addiction and Kitty was to return to the infirmary on many occasions to have pins and needles taken from all parts of her body.

The intense pain resulted in many violent convulsions and her life frequently hung by a thread. Then the miraculous happened. During hospitalisation she met an old playmate from her days at Arnold whom she had not seen since living at Nottingham. He had just had an eye removed, but with his other he soon fell for the charms of pathetic Kitty, who was now 20 years old. Later she confided that he had promised that even if she lost every limb from her body he would love all that was left. Their relationship blossomed into a successful marriage and Kitty conquered her reliance upon sharp objects.

Amazingly her body grew strong again and in between bearing 19 children, of whom all but one reached maturity, Kitty carried the post each day by foot from Arnold to Nottingham. She became a popular and familiar figure, always dressed in a small bonnet and a man's spencer (a short jacket) which was made of drab cloth. A coarse woollen petticoat, worsted stockings and strong shoes completed her ensemble and she carried the huge leather mail bag over her shoulder with vigour.

After her husband died in 1814 Kitty went to live with friends in Derbyshire. She presumably lived to a good age and is buried in that county, her terrible childhood long forgotten.

The Rufford Mine Disaster

ON the night of 7th February 1913, 14 brave men were killed in a pit disaster at the Bolsover Colliery Company's new Rufford Sinkings on Lord Savile's estate. This tragedy was yet another addition to the long list of mine disasters, but according to reports of that time it was unique in the annals of pit sinking and its terrible results plunged Nottinghamshire into deepest mourning.

The cause of the accident was simple enough. A faulty nail caused the awning of a temporary rain shelter to fall on the head of the engine-man, Sidney Brown, just as the swiftly revolving drums drew a seven ton steel water barrel from the shaft. He was therefore unable to check the barrel, which ascended to the headgear. Here a patent appliance, known as the Ormerod hook, failed to hold the heavy water-laden barrel, which hurtled at great speed back down into the workings.

On a platform, 145 ft below, a gang of 18 men was at work. The barrel smashed into them with terrific force, instantly killing 13 and seriously injuring another man who later died in Mansfield Hospital. The other four escaped by hanging on to the debris floating in the icy cold water at the bottom of the shaft.

As so often occurs at such times, the heroism and

kindness of other workers was tremendous. Immediately, without thought of their own safety, men went down the mine shaft to rescue their colleagues and tend the wounded. Mr Cook, the master sinker, with some 35 years of mining experience, declared, 'I never meant to sleep until I got the poor fellows out.' The Mayor of Mansfield, Mr J. P. Houlton JP, paid a high tribute at the inquest to both Mr Cook and his mates Dick Barratt and John Clarke for their bravery in dealing with the situation. 'It speaks volumes for the devotion, self sacrifice and comradeship of the sinkers, that when the appeal went forth for volunteers to undertake this hazardous task there was a ready and ungrudging response.'

All through the weekend the men worked night and day to cope with the rapid influx of water in the shaft, but eventually a diver had to be sent down. It was not until the following Tuesday evening that the first two bodies were recovered. Drags had to be used to draw the remainder of the men from their watery grave.

The Sunday following the recovery of the bodies resounded with prayers for the dead and those they had left behind to mourn their loss. Messages of sympathy were sent by the Secretary of State and other important national and local figures and a fund of £2,000 was eventually raised for the dead miners' families.

The inquest was opened at Mansfield on 12th February and closed on 26th February. The verdict? Accidental death with no criminal blame attached to any person.

This verdict was not in accord with the findings of HM Inspector of Mines, Mr W. Walker, whose report and conclusions were eventually issued in a White Paper. It was stated that since the accident a better hook had been designed and tested, and although the margin of safety was nearly doubled, it still did not appear to Mr Walker to be sufficient for safe working in a sinking pit.

Although the whole of the arrangements of the surface and the shafts were all that could be desired, it was regrettable, said Mr Walker, that the winding engine-man had erected and continued to use so flimsy and dangerous a covering over his chair, and also that the manager and engine-wright had allowed it to be used. They were all guilty of an error of judgement which was directly the cause of the loss of 14 lives. Walker expressed the hope that the lessons learned in that accident would result in management ensuring that nothing of a temporary or insecure character was used about the winding arrangements at this and other sinking pits in the future.

On the 13th, 14th and 15th February the families and friends of the victims went to the churchyard to bury their men. Andrew and Frank Bagnall, Thomas Jordan, Joseph Battney, John Tomilson, Jesse Hart, Henry Scott, Walter Storey, John Knowles, Herbert Woodward, James Wigman, Patrick Mulligan, William Hollins and Frederick Paddon were to enter the ground for the last time. Their conveyance was not the customary lift which they had used all their working lives but a coffin, and all the time the furnaces and grates of England demanded to be fed, oblivious of the cost.

One Month with Nurse Thatcher

WHEN home confinements were normal practice it was customary for many middle class families to employ a nurse for one month to live with the family and care for the mother and her baby.

A new father wrote an article in the 26th February 1881 edition of the *Nottingham Society* complaining of the enormous appetite of their 'monthly nurse', Mrs Thatcher, who settled upon his house like a single-minded locust.

This woman had a rapacious appetite and continuously gorged herself on snacks, colossal amounts of victuals and tumblers of alcohol without suffering any ill effects. The 'British Husband' appears to have spent much of his time anticipating the woman's death or at least discomfort from her continuous gluttony during her terrible stay under his roof. However, Nurse Thatcher was made of stronger metal.

He wrote the article to alert the whole of Nottingham to the culinary insatiability of the dreadful woman. 'I certify, on my word of honour as a British Husband Housekeeper, that the following copy is correctly taken from my wife's entries in my pocket-book, checked impartially by the cook's slate.' He then proceeds to list a sample menu for a typical day during Nurse Thatcher's sojourn with his household.

> '7 am. Breakfast — tea, buttered toast, half-quartern loaf, bloaters, three eggs, and bacon.
> 9.30 am. First morning snack — mutton chops, glass of sherry and plate of biscuits.
> 11 am. Second morning snack — a basin of tea and a sponge cake, with tumbler of brandy and water.
> 12.45 pm. Dinner — a roast loin of mutton and mashed potatoes, with ale spiced and warmed; after dinner a tumbler of hot gin and water.
> 3 pm. Afternoon snack — a glass of sherry and plate of biscuits.
> 4.30 pm. Tea and pile of muffins.
> 7 pm. Evening snack — stewed cheese, toast and a tumbler of brandy and water.
> 9 pm. Supper — juicy steak and two glasses of beer, stewed cheese and tumbler of gin and water.'

'At 4.30 am on the morning of Tuesday my wife was awakened by hearing the nurse walking up and down the room, and sighing bitterly. The following conversation then took place between them: My Wife: "Are you ill?" Mrs Thatcher: "No, hungry."

'I can certify the above list correctly, and even moderately, represents Mrs Thatcher's daily bill of fare for one month. I can assert, from my own observation, that every dish, at every hour of the day, which went up to her full, invariably came down from her empty.

'After the breakfast, the two morning snacks, and the dinner — all occurring within the space of six hours — she could move about the room with unimpeded freedom of action; could keep my wife and the baby in a state of the strictest discipline; could curtsey magnificently when the unoffending master, whom she was eating out of house and home, entered the room, preserving her colour, her equilibrium, and her staylaces, when she sank down, and when she swelled up again, without the apparent vestige of an effort.

'During the month of her devastating residence under my roof, she had 248 meals, and she went out of the house no larger and no redder than she came into it.

'I leave this case in the hands of the medical and the married public. I present it as a problem to physiological science. I offer it as a warning to British husbands with limited incomes. While I write these lines — while I give my married countrymen this friendly caution — my wife is weeping over the tradesmen's bills; my children are on half allowance of food; my cook is worked off her legs through having to do housemaid's work in addition to her own; and my purse is empty.

'Young husbands and Nottingham friends about to marry, commit to memory the description here given of my late monthly nurse, who is at the present time perambulating this town, "seeking whom she may devour".

'Avoid a tall and dignified woman, with a flowing style of conversation, and impressive manners. Beware, my struggling fellow toilers along the heavily-taxed highways of domestic happiness — beware of Mrs Thatcher!!'

The Mothering Sunday Revival

THE origins of Mothering Sunday go back to ancient times when the religious festival of visiting the Mother Church was held on the fourth Sunday in Lent. It was also customary for children living away from home to call on their mother and bring her small gifts.

Over the centuries the custom lost its popularity, until the early years of the 20th century when it was reinstated through the efforts of Miss Constance Penswick Smith, the daughter of the vicar of Coddington, near Newark.

Constance was one of seven children and her four brothers entered the church ministry. She was a home loving girl, who until the age of twelve was educated at the vicarage by her mother. She then attended a dame school at Newark and later went to a school for young ladies at Nottingham.

After finishing her education she spent two years as a governess in Germany. Upon her return to England she trained as a chemist's dispenser and in 1905 was employed by a Nottingham skin specialist.

In 1907 Constance learned that the Americans had started their own Mother's Day which was completely removed from the Church. They were also trying to bring the custom to England. In retaliation against what she considered to be a profane practice, she commenced her own campaign to revive the traditional Mothering Sunday and formed the Mothering Sunday Movement. She eventually quit her dispensing job and moved into a house in Regent Street, Nottingham, which was to be the movement's headquarters. Later everything was moved over to Marston Road, where she remained until she died.

In 1914 the United States Congress stipulated that the second Sunday in May was to be designated Mother's Day. Miss Penswick Smith was undeterred by this announcement and continued with her hard work and the writing of a book entitled *The Revival of Mothering Sunday* which was published in 1921.

She canvassed and bombarded local places of worship with her literature and leaflets and gradually the tradition was reinstated. Her family connections with the Church helped, but her energy and enthusiasm was phenomenal.

Whilst working as a dispenser Constance boarded at the Girls' Friendly Society in Nottingham, whose warden was Miss Ellen Porter. The women became lifelong friends and eventually shared a home together, with Ellen assisting with the campaign work which was totally financed by Constance.

Constance wrote Mothering Sunday services and hymns and designed special cards for Sunday school children to colour and give to their mothers. Stories and plays promoting the tradition were written and mailings sent as far away as Australia and New Zealand. Much support was given by the Penswick Smith brothers and also by Rev Killer, vicar of St Cyprian's church in Carlton, Nottingham.

Killer wrote several hymns for the festival and in 1936, when the new St Cyprian's was dedicated, a canister holding leaflets and books regarding the festival was buried under the altar.

The movement's leaflets were very stirring. The one for Mothering Sunday, 7th March 1937 urged everyone to

'Take part in this festival of our home blessed by Mother Church, and so help to strengthen the family life of our nation.'

The reinstated traditions of the fourth Sunday in Lent were very pleasant. Young children would gather bunches of primroses and violets, which were taken to church for blessing and presented to their mothers. Violets were considered to be emblems of a mother's love and it was said that 'He who goes a-mothering finds violets in the lane.'

It was also customary to eat little simnel or 'Ladoma' cakes on this day, the word 'simnel' probably derived from the Latin simila, fine flour.

Children who were away from home in service were given a day's holiday to visit their mother. They would take with them simple gifts which they had made throughout the year, perhaps an embroidered sampler or cushion or a little wooden box.

Nottinghamshire had its traditional Mothering Sunday dish of 'fermity', made from soaked whole grains of corn, boiled in water, drained and mixed with hot spiced milk.

'Clipping the Church' was another custom often performed at this time of year, when the congregation joined hands and encircled the church, 'clipping' or embracing their place of worship.

After years of unceasing hard work the Misses Penswick Smith and Porter placed Mothering Sunday back on the calendar. Constance worked vigorously until her death on 10th June 1938. Ellen Porter continued to dispatch leaflets and other literature until her own death four years later.

Despite the continued efforts of Miss Penswick Smith's family to promote the religious aspect of Mothering Sunday, they have been unable to stem the change to the present highly commercial 'Mother's Day'. It is sad to think that there are now very few violets growing along the banks of the country lanes where children once went a-mothering, seeking simple emblems of their mother's love.

Putting the Pig on Harrison

THE Nottingham Race Course has seen many fortunes won and lost, but according to the *Nottingham Journal* the race between Granny from Belper and Harrison from Nottingham on 21st April 1773 caused many folk to risk losing more than their proverbial shirts on this 'dead cert'.

Fifteen thousand very excited people from all over the country converged upon the track to see these two great runners compete for a purse of £200, which in those days was an enormous prize. They had to run ten miles, which was five times round the race course, and they had to run naked.

Harrison, the local lad, was the favourite and his backers were so certain of his supremacy that according to the *Journal*, 'Many of them sold their beds, cows and swine, to raise money to make bets; and others pawned their wives' wedding rings for the same purpose; for, as the odds were seven to four and three to two, in favour of Harrison, the temptation became so much the stronger, and very considerable bets were laid: the highest odds we hear of, were £100 laid by a gentleman in the Stand, to 30.'

At two o'clock the competitors, stripped of their clothes, were poised at the touchline and were soon streaking down the track at a swinging pace. Granny held the lead for seven miles and looked set to win. Doubtless Harrison's backers were rehearsing their excuses to their deprived wives between screaming for their man, when their prayers were answered.

Fourth time around the track Granny fell and injured his right leg. Harrison gained nearly 50 yards. Applause thundered throughout the race course but Granny would not give up. He pushed forward in the downhill section, but stumbled and almost fell to the ground, totally winded. 'His courage and strength then failing, he gave up the contest, with tears flowing from his eyes.' The race had taken 56 minutes and two seconds.

The lucky punters celebrated with good Nottingham Ale before redeeming their goods from the pawnbrokers who, win or lose, always thanked God for the gambling man.

Mad, Bad and Dangerous to Know

IT was Lady Caroline Lamb, the wife of the future Viscount Melbourne and Whig Prime Minister from 1835–1841, who wrote in her diary on the night that she first met the poet Lord Byron that he was 'mad, bad and dangerous to know.' She might have added that this applied to several others of the Byron family.

The Byrons' family home was at Newstead Abbey, which then stood on the edge of Sherwood Forest. The abbey had been found by Henry II circa 1170 to house the Austin canons. After suffering at the hands of Henry VIII both the abbey and Hucknall church were purchased by Sir John Byron and it became a private house in 1550. Over the years, if local tales are to be believed, the place became chock-a-block with ghosts and apparitions including a White Lady, a Black Friar, a Goblin Friar and a Byron ancestor known as 'Sir John Byron the Little with the Big Beard.'

Byron's great-uncle William, alias 'Devil Byron', was said to be haunted by the spirit of a sister, to whom he refused to speak for many years because of a family scandal. This was despite her heartrending appeals. He was also known as 'The Wicked Lord', having killed a Nottinghamshire neighbour, Mr Chaworth from Annesley Hall, in a drunken skirmish in the Star and Garter in Pall Mall, London, on 26th January 1762. He was acquitted of

murder but found guilty of manslaughter. After paying a fine he was immediately set free and returned to Newstead, where he lived for the rest of his days in impoverished squalor and with women of a certain reputation.

William's seafaring brother, with the rank of Vice-Admiral and the reputation of a womaniser, was known as 'Foul Weather Jack'. He earned the title as on most occasions when he set to sea his ship encountered terrible storms.

'Foul Weather Jack' died in 1786 having disinherited his son, 'Mad Jack', because of his debauched lifestyle. With a passion for women and their money, young Jack Byron had run off to France with the Marquis of Carmarthen's wife and her fortune of £4,000 a year. She obtained a divorce from her husband and married 'Mad Jack' but died shortly after giving birth to their daughter Augusta.

Jack Byron returned to England and eventually met a wealthy Scottish girl, Catherine Gordon, who had an irresistible fortune of £23,000. They married in May 1785 but Catherine's money was soon eroded by her spendthrift husband and in no time she was forced to sell her family home in Scotland. She and 'Mad Jack' fled to France to escape from their creditors, but Catherine returned to England in time to give birth to her son, George Gordon, on 22nd January 1788.

The future poet's first home was a dingy, small back room off Oxford Street, London. George was born with deformed ankles and a clubfoot, which were to cause him great mental and physical pain for much of his life. Jack Byron travelled about France enjoying freedom from his responsibilities, which he celebrated in a series of brief love affairs. Shortly before George's first birthday he died. With just a small income to live off, Catherine Byron moved with her son and his nurse to better accommodation, but she became mentally unstable.

The young and fatherless Byron thus had an unstable early upbringing with a mother who was cursed with bouts of terrible temper and hysteria, interspersed with periods of more gentle behaviour. He was a beautiful plump little boy with a mop of auburn curls, and said to be the butt of cruel teasing by other children concerning his ankles and clubfoot, which caused his limping gait. His mother took him to a succession of doctors, quacks and surgeons for what often amounted to torturous treatment, which at one stage involved having his foot screwed at an angle in a wooden machine.

Byron bore the pain with great fortitude and when his Latin tutor remarked to his pupil, 'It makes me uncomfortable to see you sitting there in such pain as I know you must be suffering,' young George is said to have replied, 'Never mind me, Mr Rogers, you shall not see any signs of it in me.'

In 1798 'Devil Byron' died and George Gordon inherited at the age of ten years in default of the fifth Lord's grandson and rightful heir, who had been killed in Corsica.

The sixth Lord Byron and his mother lost no time in going to Nottinghamshire, where they were horrified to find the Abbey in a hopeless state of repair. Reception rooms were used as hay stores, the roofs were leaking. There was very little furniture as anything of value had been seized by the 'Wicked Lord's' creditors. The estate had long been neglected with its farm buildings abandoned and fields and parkland without stock.

Despite the dereliction young Byron and Catherine were enchanted by the peace and natural beauty which engulfed Newstead. They were especially fond of the large quiet lake which had once been the scene of the fifth Lord's strange passion for mock 'sea' battles. He had fake fortresses and castles built along its shores and mimic fleets sailed its waters firing off salvoes of destruction.

When mother and son stood together beside the lake on their first visit after the inheritance, they must surely have known about the unsubstantiated stories of treasure said to be buried in its waters. The rumours may have stemmed from the great brass eagle with wide spread wings, standing on a pedestal, that was fished up from the deepest part of its waters. It had doubtless served as a stand or reading desk in the abbey chapel, to hold a folio bible or missal. The sacred relic was sent to a brazier to be cleaned and it was discovered that the pedestal was hollow. Inside were a number of parchment deeds belonging to the abbey, bearing the seals of Edward III and Henry VIII. The eagle was transferred to the church at Southwell.

Catherine Byron stayed on at Newstead and her son lodged with a family in St James's Street, Nottingham, where he was taught the classics. He was later educated at Harrow, his mother having obtained a pension from the civil list which paid for his school fees.

Byron is said to have shown signs of his future talents at a very young age, during an early visit to Newstead, as remembered in a tale recounted by his nurse. An elderly lady frequently visited his mother and her remarks never failed to irritate the little boy. The old lady had some strange ideas and one concerned the soul, which she thought took flight to the moon after death as a first stopping place before flying on to Heaven. One day the visitor had especially annoyed little George who flew into a violent rage. His nurse enquired, 'Well, my little hero, what's the matter with you now?' The peeved child broke into the following doggerel lines, which he frequently repeated and called his 'first dash into poetry.'

> 'In Nottinghamshire town, very near to Swine Green,
> Lives as curst an old lady as ever was seen;
> And when she does die, which I hope will be soon,
> She firmly believes she will go to the moon.'

Whilst living at Newstead, Lord Byron found a large human skull. He assumed this to belong to some 'jolly soul of a friar' who had lived there before the Dissolution of the Monasteries. He converted this cranium to a drinking vessel which he called 'Friar Tuck' and sent it off to London to be mounted. On its return to Newstead, Byron instituted a new order at the abbey, making himself Grand Master, or Abbot of the Skull. The twelve members of the order and their 'Abbot' wore black gowns when they attended their chapter meetings. The skull-goblet was filled with claret at their ceremonies and handed amongst the fraternity, who were said to have had a great deal of fun at the expense of the rightful owner of the head. The skull is said to have been eventually buried beneath the floor of the chapel at Newstead Abbey.

Byron had been warned in his youth by a fortune teller to 'Beware your 37th birthday'. In 1823 he became involved in the Greek struggle of independence and he died at Missolonghi on 19th April 1824, while training troops. He was 36 years old. A period of three weeks mourning was decreed for the dead poet. Following an autopsy his heart and brain were placed in separate urns. The lungs were buried at a funeral service in the local church of St Spiridion on 22nd April.

Byron had announced on his death bed that he wished to be buried in England, and so the body was embalmed in a casket containing 180 gallons of spirits and was shipped to England, where it arrived on 29th June 1824.

The Dean of Westminster refused to have Byron buried in the Abbey and he was made similarly unwelcome at St Paul's. It was eventually arranged for his remains to be taken to Hucknall Torkard, Nottinghamshire, and deposited in the family vault. A huge crowd watched the small funeral procession leave London.

On the 15th July 1824 the procession reached Nottinghamshire and the noble poet rested at the Blackamoor's Head inn. Church bells tolled and special constables were shipped in to control the crowds. The following day some 40 local gentry joined the funeral courtege and Byron was laid to rest in the vaults of St Mary Magdelene in company with 15 of his ancestors and alongside the 'Wicked Lord'. The poet's coffin was draped with a velvet cloth with coronets placed at each end. On a chest enclosed inside the coffin was the inscription, 'Within this Urn are deposited the Heart, Brains etc of the deceased Lord Byron.'

However, Byron was not to lie undisturbed for rumours persisted that the body which lay in the Byron vaults at Hucknall Torkard was not that of George Gordon. Therefore in 1938 the local vicar received permission from the Home Office and the surviving Lord Byron to have the poet's tomb opened in order to record the contents.

On the 15th June a small group of people made their way down the steps which led to the vault. The floor was littered with decaying wood and scores of bones, but there was the poet's coffin, still intact and shrouded in its fraying cloth with the two coronets in situ.

The lid was carefully opened and there was Byron, 114 years into eternal rest but in a perfect state of preservation except for his hands and feet. His clubfoot had fallen off and was at the bottom of the coffin and his heart and brains remained sealed in the urn. The coffin was photographed but not its contents.

On 8th May 1969 a memorial to Lord Byron was conducted by the Dean of Westminster, having been petitioned by the Poetry Society of Great Britain.

Of Flood and Tempest

THE river Trent flows through the centre of Nottinghamshire, the great highway for goods and merchandise in times past. Today banks are lined with power stations, which continue to expand in number. In the past mills throbbed along its banks, whilst willows grown for cricket bats and basket making have had their roots nourished by the old river. This watercourse provides the main source of drainage for the county and has a flood plain two miles wide in some places.

The river has been the source of many terrible floodings. Towards the end of the 16th century a storm devastated Wilford and Bridgford, which lie to the south of the river Trent. What was described as 'marvellous tempest of thunder' was said to have beaten down all the houses and churches; 'the bells were cast to the outside of the churchyards, and some webs of lead rolled 400 ft into the field, writhen like a pair of gloves.' The river flooded the area for a quarter of a mile and trees were uprooted. 'A child was taken forth of a man's hand, two spear lengths high, and carried an hundred ft, and then let fall, whereby his arm was broken, and so he died; five or six were slain. There fell some hailstones that were 15 inches about.'

One very strange event which was known locally as the 'Terrible Tempest' is said to have happened in November 1785. The day started well with a clear sky and agreeable temperature for the time of year. At about eleven o'clock in the morning the sky became very overcast, before it started to rain in torrents and the wind roared. Suddenly, around two o'clock in the afternoon, everything was hushed in a deathly calm. People from just outside Sneinton reported a weird and frightening sight at about four o'clock.

An immense water spout was proceeding from a dense cloud about a quarter of a mile south of the river Trent, and moving slowly towards it. People standing within its path said that as the spout passed over, it bent the branches of strong trees almost to the ground.

As the cloud got nearer to the river the water became strongly attracted by it. When it crossed the Trent the cloud or spout was only some 30 ft from the surface of the water, which heaved and tossed in great agitation. Sightseers standing on the Trent Bridge described the phenomenon as being 'a huge black inverted cone, terminating nearly in a point, and in which they perceived very plainly a whirling spiral motion, accompanied with a rumbling noise, like distant thunder.' It was calculated that the middle of the column was nearly 20 ft in diameter.

After passing the river it ascended slowly and majestically in a north-easterly direction and hit Sneinton with a vengeance. Thatched roofs were completely ripped from cottages and barns and tossed into the air like pieces of paper. Apple trees were uprooted. One with a four ft diameter trunk was broken off close to the ground as easily as snapping a twig. The column flattened a large and substantial barn, devastated the adjoining house and tore up a huge sycamore tree. The rain poured down and joined the noise of the raging wind, 'and the terrific aspect of the yet undissolved waterspout, floating as it were, a little over [the spectators'] heads, produced a feeling of alarm and confusion which was impossible to describe.'

Several of the Sneinton folk were thrown into the middle of a hedge and one 14 year old boy was carried up and over it and landed uninjured in the adjoining field.

The drinkers in a nearby public house all complained of terrible sensations in their heads as the storm passed over, and their discomfort lasted several hours. Flashes of lightning darted from the tornado whilst it was passing over the fields, and as it rolled over the Colwick Hills the people in the tavern saw it contract and expand in a strange manner, as though it had been under the influence of electrical attraction and repulsion from some extraneous forces.

In times when winters were very severe the river was liable to break its banks when the thaw melted the ice and snow and swelled its waters to bursting point. In February 1795 there was a terrible flooding of the river Trent which inundated most of the valleys of Staffordshire, Derbyshire and Nottinghamshire.

On Christmas Eve 1794 there had been an extremely harsh frost, followed at intervals over many days by severe snow storms. Everywhere remained frozen until around the 9th February when a rapid thaw set in. The river Trent was sent into a whirling flooded frenzy, carrying away vast sheets of half melted snow, rails, timber, posts, houses and sheep. It even flooded the lower parts of Nottingham where the residents of Narrow Marsh were imprisoned in their homes for two days and nights with the water lapping to a depth of three ft.

The canal banks were washed away and many cattle and sheep perished. West Bridgford lost 19 beasts and 30 sheep and at Lenton upwards of 400 sheep were drowned. The new 'Ten-Arch Bridge' or Trent Bridge was rendered useless. An eye-witness wrote, 'in short the scene the Trent presented, bearing down in its mighty stream, horses and sheep, haystacks and trees, and farm produce of all kinds, was amply sufficient to show the unprecedented extent of the calamity.'

Nineteen years later to the day, it seemed likely to happen again, when the 'Thirteen Weeks Frost' set in. The river Trent was completely sealed with a thick sheet of ice.

Hundreds of skaters, sliders and others of all ages and states of fitness were to be seen daily enjoying their new sport. Great fires blazed for hours at different points between Wilford Ferry and the Trent Bridge.

There was a great fear that once the thaw set in the river would flood as it had done on so many previous occasions. A mechanical device was set up on the Trent Bridge so that once the temperature rose above freezing, large balls of cast iron with ropes attached could be crashed onto the ice, which could then be carted away. This would preserve the bridge and lessen the risk of inundation by securing a free channel through the arches for the rising water.

On 7th February there was a slight thaw, although followed by renewed frost, but whilst conditions were good the huge balls pounded the ice and large chunks of the stuff were transported to safety. Occasionally the piers of the bridge were shaken as great ice floes knocked against their structure. The customary huge crowd of people gathered to watch the work and, if lucky, witness at first hand any accidents. The bridge was saved but the meadows resembled an inland sea.

The flood of 4th December 1910 was again the result of thawing snow and the improvements in drainage and dredging of the river bed proved totally inadequate. The floods continued to rise between Nottingham and Gainsborough and one of the most remarkable features was the flooding of the Midland Railway line from beyond Attenborough to the centre of the bridge of the Nottingham Midland station. All trains between Nottingham and Trent had to plough their way for five miles through water three to four ft deep in places, yet every locomotive got through safely.

The Trent is now a tamed river, its banks fortified by flood banks, piles, stones, cement and even sunken barges. It is a lifeline which has brought wealth to the region, and remains Nottinghamshire's vital artery.

Beating the Bounds

NOTTINGHAMSHIRE has always participated in the traditional custom of Beating the Bounds at Rogationtide, and the custom of walking the boundaries still exists in some of its parishes.

The Rogation Days which occur before Ascension Day are a survival of two ancient Roman customs, Ambarvalia and Terminalia, which occurred in May and June when sacrificial animals were taken around fields and boundaries and offered to Mars in exchange for good crops. Like so many pagan customs, these were absorbed into Christian festivals and therefore, three days before Ascension, priests and parishioners processed their territory, carrying peeled wands and praying for blessings on the crops and at the same time the boundaries were marked. The ritual was known as 'Beating the Bounds' and was a good way for people to remember their boundaries in the days when maps were few and inaccurate and not many people could read.

At the Reformation the ceremonies and practices were deemed objectionable and were abolished and only the 'useful and harmless part of the custom retained.' Yet its observance was considered so essential that a homily was prepared for the occasion and injunctions were issued requiring that for 'the perambulation of the circuits of parishes, the people should once in the year, at the time accustomed, with the rector, vicar or curate, and the substantial men of the parish, walk about the parishes, as they were accustomed, and at their return to the church, make their common prayer.'

And so on this day the parishioners were entitled by law to trespass on lands and even enter private houses if these stood on the boundary line. If a canal was similarly cut then it was necessary for some of the parishioners to pass through the water. When a river formed a boundary the parishioners either had to pass through it in boats or some of the party stripped and swum in it, or boys were thrown into it.

The young children had the boundary marks impressed upon them by being bumped or whipped at each important point. They were thrown into ponds and rivers, forced to climb over roofs of dwellings which straddled the boundary and bumped upon boundary marker stones. In later years should any boundary dispute arise, they would have painful memories of just where the line of demarcation lay.

In 1874 Alderman Whitehead issued a pamphlet describing the perambulation around Nottingham as he knew it.

'On Perambulation Day the committee and other burgesses, with axes, crow bars, shovels and other implements, walked over the various lands subject to common-right, claimed to have a road through any buildings recognised as encroachments, and by the execution of something like Lynch Law prevented these encroachments increasing.

'One year in particular, about 1832, was memorable for the incidents the perambulation produced. Assembling at the Three Crowns in Parliament Street, we proceeded to the corner of Park Row. Each building there was entered by a door, and if there was no second door a hole was quickly made in the opposite wall. Then Chimley's buildings at the top of Derby road were similarly visited.

Passing thence to the site of the present General Cemetery, the formidable party marched down the fields in a line with Back Lane (now Wollaren Street) to Dr Lavendar's close, the site of Whitehall's factory (at the corner of Goldsmith Street).

'A barn in this field was gently treated, the door being merely opened and closed again because "the doctor" in antique wig and George III costume, stood on the opposite side of the way in the recess which still exists. His housekeeper [stood] by his side in front of them on the low wall, bearing trays loaded with smoking punch and rich plum cake. Everyone being cheerfully and freely supplied with as much as he could eat and drink, the "chairman" of the committee gave the order to march up Larkdale, now Waverley Street, passing the old red brick house that stood at the corner of Roper's Close, now Goldsmith Street, on which was generally painted by some devout hand, "The Way to Hell, to the Races."

'We crossed the road to the old cottage owned by Mr Duggan, an Irish gentleman who had obtained possession by marrying an English lady.

'Mr Duggan, dressed in a blouse fantastically braided like that of a stage brigand, flew into a passion, brandished a wide mouthed blunderbuss in our faces, and swore he would blow out the brains of anyone who dared to trespass upon the domain he claimed exclusively as his own. The surprise was unexpected and the party retreated with great precipitancy and in much disorder. On rallying a council was called and it was agreed to depute some three or four to reason with the enraged gentleman. The result was a truce, and the deputation being allowed to pass through the house and grounds to perpetuate the right of the burgesses. The rest, with the tag-rag and bobtail, were content merely to look over the gate.'

Not all parishes inspected their boundaries during Rogation, for R. Mellows recorded in his book *Then and Now*, published in the 19th century, that West Bridgford had its bounds beaten by the Mickletorn Jury every 4th September.

The Jury was sworn in on the previous night and set off from the Town Hall at eight o'clock the next morning. Their course was about 15 miles and they usually returned to the Town Hall at eight o'clock that evening to record their proceedings.

The Jurymen divided, one part taking a boat from the canal, going down the Trent, then walking by and touching the boundary stone on Barrow Hill Farm, going by old Lady Bay Bridge and the Brook Bridge. The other part of the Jury went to the west and the south by the 'borough proper' boundary, extending to the 'Stone Man' on the Melton Road, the two parties meeting up at the Town Arms.

Each year they would sing a different 'Mickletorn Jury' song and the chorus of the long entertainment for 1850, composed by Mr W. Bradbury, their poet, went:

> 'Shoulder your spades and march away,
> The sun shines bright, 'tis a glorious day!
> Our Foreman's the King, whom we all obey,
> We serve on the Mickletorn Jury.'

And what about modern Nottinghamshire? In some places the old boundary customs exist. For instance, each Rogation Monday (commonly known as Mickleton Monday) at Gringley on the Hill, a procession climbs to the top of Beacon Hill to ask for God's blessing on the surrounding countryside. At Tithby-cum-Cropwell Butler, weather permitting, the parish priest leads his congregation on Rogation Sunday, together with the church choir from Crompwell Bishop, to bless the local farms.

The Whipping Judge

ENORMOUS personal powers were once vested in magistrates, who could, at their individual discretion, inflict severe punishments in the name of law and order. In 1761 Robert Huish, JP and Mayor of Nottingham, ordered a punishment for Jos Hollingworth which seems out of proportion for his crime. In fact even in those days he was compelled to issue a public statement to vindicate his judicial conduct.

Apparently on 8th August Hollingworth had called on the house of this Justice of the Peace who lived at Goose Gate and knocked violently upon his door. Accompanied by a large gang of friends, he had come to demand the reason why Huish had put him in the stocks. The JP replied, 'I told him I never did; nor did I know who it was that put him in. He told me I lied, for he knew that I had put him in.'

Hollingworth was then told to go about his business or it would be the worse for him. The reply was 'He said that he valued me not, nor did he care for either mayor or horse, or what such scoundrels could do at him, for that he had been in the Bridewell at Southwell and at Mr Parr's.' Mr Parr was the Governor of the County Gaol, Nottingham.

The mayor sent for a police constable, who took half an hour to turn up, and the two men were obliged to remain arguing at the mayor's front door for that duration.

Gradually a large crowd began to form and word soon got around the town to go to Goose Gate if anyone wanted a bit of fun.

Hollingworth was ranting 'Such scoundrels as Alderman Butler, and altogether, I don't value what any of you can do to me, d--n you, I value you not.'

The mayor fuelled the situation by demanding a shilling fine the first time Hollingworth swore at him, it being within a magistrate's powers to make such an imposition. This penalty was useless for 'He d-d me, and could not find one.'

The situation attracted an audience of several hundred, most of whom stood laughing at the mayor and shouting advice to Hollingworth.

Eventually Constable Billings turned up and according to the JP-mayor was 'confounded at what he (Hollingworth) said and did; and though I exhorted him several times to go away and be quiet, it was to no purpose; for he said he had a tongue, and no horse nor mayor should prevent him saying and doing what he pleased.'

The mayor lost his temper and ordered the constable to place the man in the stocks, which were situated in Nottingham Market Place, near the Malt Cross. Hollingworth was dragged off by the scruff of his collar, followed by the crowd like the Pied Piper of Hamelin. In no time at all he had escaped from his rustic prison, possibly helped by his large number of sympathisers.

When Huish found out he fell into a terrible temper and demanded that Billings should scour the town and return the prisoner in great haste if he wanted to keep his job. The PC was soon back at the mayor's front door with Hollingworth writhing and swearing in his clasp and the crowd cheering and jeering. Hollingworth was then ordered to be taken to the dungeons in the House of Correction where he stayed for a week and was fed on a diet of bread and water.

Robert Huish takes up the story, 'I ordered the keeper of

the House of Correction to whip him there, and then have him put into a cart and drawn by my door, for an example, and to terrify anybody whatever from vilifying and degrading magistracy as he did, and from doing the like in the future! And let him be drawn through the Market, that the country might see him.'

He explained that he had issued this statement to tell the public why he had delivered this punishment — 'As I had not any concern in putting him in the stocks the first time.' The mayor did it because of 'The regard I had in supporting the dignity of magistracy, and prevent for the future any contempt that might be thrown upon it. I say, if the public are offended, or have the least reason to find fault why such a man, who pays no regard to our laws, nor to the power or dignity of magistracy — but shall be suffered or allowed to vilify and abuse in the manner he did, before several hundreds of witnesses.

'To satisfy them, I acknowledge his being whipped in the House of Correction and exposing him in the manner I did, was for abusing me at my door, before hundreds of country and townspeople, and for telling me I lie. . . .

'And as for his being kept in the House of Correction for seven days, he swore several oaths and curses before me, and when I asked him to pay for them, it was impossible for him to pay who had no money.

'All these and many more provocations which I was obliged to stand and hear (as I could not get a constable for more than half an hour) was the cause of what I ordered to be done to him, and also for appearing before me drunk.'

We can only assume that Hollingworth learned his lesson and stayed away from the mayor's front door in future.

Riding The Stang

IT was customary in many parts of England until the end of the 19th century, and later in some areas, for rural communities to punish errant husbands and wives who offended in any way against the village standards of honesty or morality, with a special emphasis on sexual offences or disharmony. In Nottinghamshire the punishment appears to have been reserved mainly for wife beaters.

The tradition had several names, including Skimmington, Riding Skimmerton, Rough Music, the Ran-Dan and Riding the Stang, the latter being well known in several Nottinghamshire villages. By whatever name, the treatment usually had the desired effect of humiliating the offender and possibly driving him or her away.

It is believed that Rough Music is an ancient custom, quite likely stemming from pagan times when people believed that fertility was undivided. The power which controlled the crops controlled mankind. If relationships between the sexes were not good it would have implications upon the fertility of the land.

The simple but harsh treatment was carried out at night when the villagers paraded through the streets playing their 'rough music' on tin kettles, horns and saucepans or anything of a percussive nature. They were usually accompanied by an effigy of the miscreant which they pushed in a cart. The onomatopoeic 'ran, tan, tan' refrain blended beautifully with the rhythm of the so-called musical instruments.

Amidst the din of the 'music', verses would be shouted out referring to the incident which had necessitated the punishment. The following are a few examples of Stang Riding doggerel said to have been used in Nottinghamshire:

'With a ran, dan, dan,
Sing o' my owd tin frying pan,
A brazened-faced villain has been paying his best wo-man;
He neither paid her wi' stick, stake or a stower,
But he up wi' his fisses an' he knocked her ower.
With a ran, dan, dan.'

In this instance 'paying' meant hitting or beating. Another verse on the same theme was:

'Mestur So-and-so has been beating his good woman,
We doesn't know the reason for what nor for why;
But its supposed she wannut eat
Cold cabbage when she's dry.
To my ran, tan, tan.
He paid her head, he paid her side,
An' that's the reason wey do ride,
With a ran, tan, tan.'

The phrase 'wannut eat cold cabbage when she's dry' meant the woman would not tamely accept the storm of abuse her husband bestowed with his tongue, but retaliated in kind; hence the 'paying' process given by the brutish husband.

Similar treatment was doled out to a wife beater in a village some three miles from Southwell in 1830. After going around the village the effigy was brought to the door of the house of the offending husband and set on fire.

Members of the Caunton Women's Institute recorded two verses of the 'Rang-Tang' in *The Nottinghamshire Village Book* which was published in 1989. Some of the older women could remember the custom being enacted. However it would appear that on this occasion the villagers condoned 'Hodge Podge's' behaviour because he had a nagging wife. Perhaps both man and wife were put to shame.

> 'There is a man in our town
> Hodge Podge is his name.
> He's been beating his good wife
> Don't you think this a shame?
>
> It's not because she's icy
> It's not because she's lame.
> She wants to wear the breeches
> That's her little game.'

It was generally supposed that if the Ran-dan was performed on three successive evenings, proceedings could not be taken against anyone. In his book *Notes About Nottinghamshire*, C. Brown wrote of this belief, 'Those who get up the entertainment may say this to induce hangers-back to come forward, but most people think, if it is properly gone through, they are safe from any consequences attending a breach of the peace.'

The Roeites of Calverton

JOHN Roe was baptised at Calverton church on 16th July 1732 and brought up in the faith of the Church of England. In the middle of the 18th century many of the local parishioners seem to have fallen out with their vicar, Rev Maurice Pugh, and it may have been this which led to the formation of the Calverton Roeites in about 1785.

The movement was formed by John Roe and styled loosely on the Quaker religion. They sometimes referred to themselves as 'Reformed Quakers', but were popularly known as 'Deformed Quakers'.

A Mr J. Morley of Calverton had a letter printed in the *Nottingham Journal* dated 31st March 1787 stating that he had heard Pastor Roe preach some 20 times. He stated that:

> 'Their religion, in short, is a heap of inconsistencies promiscuously jumbled together, and their preaching an invariable compound of railing, absurdity, Billingsgate and blackguardism. . . . They affirm that John Roe, their founder, holds himself as the only true prophet since the days of the Apostles, and he bitterly inveighs against all denominations, and d--ns the world in a bag. . . . And I need not hesitate to aver, that the wickedness, blasphemy, and abomination delivered from Roe's pulpit, are without parallel.'

The Roeites had a strange attitude towards marriage, which was not solemnised by a traditional wedding ceremony. There was to be no courtship and marriage had to be by ballot. A jury of twelve members was selected, who had to declare if they knew of any objectionable matters regarding the parties. It was especially important that they knew of no courtship between any candidates. If all was well at that stage, lots were cast for wedlock and all drawn cards had to be honoured, no matter how preposterous the result.

Resulting from this tenet two of their members, 'Mrs' Roe, the putative wife of Pastor Roe and her sister 'Mrs' Bush were jailed for twelve years for their faith. Both women's cases were similar.

Mrs Bush became pregnant soon after her 'marriage' and the overseer of the parish determined to make her feel the exercise of his authority. Obviously the parish authorities did not recognise the Roeite 'marriages', but as a single woman Mrs Bush's child would be a burden on the ratepayers. He accordingly took her to a magistrate, to compel her to name the father of her child, but she declared that she was a married woman. By naming the father of the child, he would have been forced to maintain it rather than the parish. She was adamant in her refusal to comply with the magistrate's orders and so was driven knee-deep in snow to Southwell House of Correction, where under the care of keeper Adams, a man known for his sadistic cruelty, she gave birth in a room with an unglazed window, through which the snow flakes blew onto her bed of straw.

In time she was sent home but soon received a citation from an ecclesiastic court, which she ignored. She was carted off to Nottingham County Gaol, to join Mrs Roe, and although every Parliamentary and other effort was made to gain the sisters' freedom, the answer was invariably the same. The children must be fathered, and the request was always refused.

The two women languished in gaol and the Bishop of York determined that in order to prevent them from becoming Roeite martyrs, which would do considerable damage to the Church of England, he would connive at their release.

In 1798, when part of the gaol was being rebuilt, the doors of the women's cells were left open and heavy hints made that no-one would see them escape. The sisters took advantage of the situation and the next day the gaoler packed up their goods and collected his fees.

The historian Blackner wrote, 'Although it is impossible not to sympathise with these objects of spiritual vengeance, in the sufferings they endured, yet we must condemn the prejudice which gave these sufferings birth. Often has the writer of these pages heard these women sigh for liberty, and, with the same breath, glory in the persecution they underwent; as though they expected their heroism to be the title-page to eternal fame. But how vain is that heroism which brings nothing but trouble in its train, and which holds up bad example as a mirror to public view.'

The movement appears to have confined itself to Calverton, where Pastor John Roe preached until he reached the age of 91 years. He was a small, venerable looking man, with shoulder length hair the colour of driven snow. Being the keystone of the movement, numbers slowly dwindled after his death.

The chapel where he preached was no more than a barn and was eventually taken over by the Primitive Methodists when the small number of Roeites could no longer maintain the building. It was sold in 1907 and the sect's burial ground has now been completely covered over.

John Roe's name also lives on horticulturally, for he developed a particularly fine plum, which is still grown locally.

The Miller of Mansfield

THIS traditional tale is based upon an old Nottingham ballad and has a plot redolent of pantomime. There is a mistaken identity and a misdemeanour, forgiveness, poverty which turns to wealth and a love so true that it will not be compromised by riches and beauty.

King Henry VIII enjoyed the chase and one day he and his noblemen were hunting in Sherwood Forest. They were so taken up with their sport that they did not notice the setting sun. Night fell and the king became detached from his party. He wandered wearily through the forest, fearing the dark and possible encounters with thieves and murderers who frequented the area. Fortunately he met a miller from Mansfield, called John Cockle. He asked the man to tell him the most direct route to fair Nottingham. The miller made it quite plain that he mistrusted his motives.

The king demanded to know upon what the miller had based his hasty judgement. He was told that he looked like a gentleman thief and if he did not make haste the miller would crack his knavish crown. The king denied all charges, but still kept his true identity concealed.

'Thou has not,' said the miller, 'one groat in thy purse; all thy inheritance lies on your back.'

Henry replied that he had sufficient gold to meet any occasion and after further assurances of innocence, the miller took the king back to his house. The miller's wife offered the visitor food and a share in her son's humble bed.

Dame Cockle supplied a hearty meal of hot bag-puddings, venison pasty and apple pies, all washed down with a large bowlful of good strong ale. The hungry king devoured the food with great gusto and proclaimed that he had never eaten anything so good and where could he purchase such delicious venison pasty?

Richard the son laughed and said that the venison cost them nothing as it was filched from the king's stock of deer which roamed about Sherwood Forest. Their guest was told to keep their guilty secret to himself and he swore his compliance.

The miller's wife busied herself with laying out fresh bed straw, on top of which she placed her best brown hempen sheets, in honour of the visitor. The men comforted themselves with several cups of 'Lamb's Wool', made from good nut brown ale and finished off with roasted crab-apples, sugar, nutmeg and ginger, and soon after were in a sound sleep.

The next morning the remainder of the hunting party searched the area for their leader and found him just as he was mounting his horse and bidding farewell to John Cockle and his family. The noblemen fell to their knees before their monarch and the Cockles quaked in their shoes. The miller was convinced that he would be hanged for questioning his majesty's character and poaching his game. He begged for mercy and the king laughed heartily and conferred a knighthood on the hospitable Miller of Mansfield.

Back in Nottingham, with plenty of ale in his belly, the king recounted his adventures, but nothing could compare with the sport he had found in the company of the Miller of Mansfield.

Sir John Cockle went about his usual work at the mill and nobody believed his newly elevated status. He still looked the same poor John, dressed in his smock and dusted with flour.

Upon the king's return to London word was sent to his newest knight and his family, desiring their company at court. The puzzled miller received the summons with caution, thinking it was some jest from his farmer friends who had been teasing him remorselessly about his supposed meeting with the king.

His fears were allayed by a token from the messenger and his assurance that he and his family were to be guests of honour at a feast. The Cockles' hearts froze. They were poor people. How should they behave? How should they get to London? The expense of it all! Dame Cockle would need a new gown. They must have good horses and serving men!

In the end the good wife trimmed up her old russet gown and they rode to court on the mill horses. Master Cockle went on ahead, cutting quite a dash with a cock's feather stuck in his hat.

The king warmly greeted the strange crew from Mansfield and bade them welcome at his court. A huge meal was set out which included a venison pasty similar to the one which had graced Dame Cockle's table. Sir John and his lady blushed with shame and their son refused to eat it exclaiming, 'Ho! Ho! 'tis knavery to eat it, and then betray it.'

After the feast it was time for dancing. The clodhoppers from Nottinghamshire provided the main entertainment for the noble assembly, who watched dumbfounded and feared for their feet as the trio charged around in shoes more fit for killing vermin than tackling a courtly dance.

As the Cockles were on the point of departure the king asked Richard if he would like to choose a wife from one of his beautiful, rich and unattached guests. The lad looked the king straight in the eye and replied, 'Jugg Grumball, sir, she's my love, and only her will I wed.'

And so they returned to their home town, John to his

new appointment which had just been awarded by the king, at a salary of £300 per annum. He was no longer to be the poor Miller of Mansfield, but instead the wealthy overseer of Sherwood Forest. Dame Cockle returned to her cooking, but as ordered by the king she used a different filling for her pasties. Richard pledged his troth to Jugg Grumball and presumably, in keeping with most traditional tales, they all lived happily ever after.

Plough Bullocks

PLOUGH Monday, for many farm labourers, was one of the most important days in their calendar. Throughout England it was on Plough Monday, being the first Monday after Epiphany, that the ploughmen returned to work after the Christmas holiday. It was also traditional centuries ago for the farmworkers and domestic servants to rise especially early on that morning. If the ploughman could get any of his tools laid out in front of the fire before the servant could boil her kettle, she forfeited her 'Shrovetide Cock' which was fattened and killed to celebrate that occasion.

Thomas Tusser (1524–1580), the rustic poet, advises:

> 'Plough Monday, next after that Twelfthtide is past,
> Bids out with the plough, the worst husband is last,
> If ploughmen get hatchet, or whip to the screen,
> Maids loseth their cock, if not water be seen.'

It is quite likely that in many areas of the country very little work was ever done on this day, for it was the custom for the men to hold wonderful revels to celebrate the start of the new working year.

Some communities did this throughout the day and night, others reserved their fun for the evening. Most of the ploughmen and boys called on the large farms and houses, plus selected public houses, with a tin to collect their largesse — miserly people were invariably punished in a most humiliating fashion. Other groups performed Mummers Plays or Plough Monday Plays, again with their collection tin at the ready. For many people this was their first introduction to 'costumed actors'. Old school log books record a high rate of absenteeism as pupils followed the jolly ploughboys, witnessing a lot of the grown ups getting up to tricks for which they as children would have received a good beating.

It was further customary for some of the ploughmen to dress up as parodies of women. In Nottinghamshire the men and boys were generally known as 'Plough Bullocks', where the air was raucous with the sound of rattling tins and the cry, 'Remember the Plough Bullocks!'

Some of the Nottinghamshire men took a great deal of time with their 'cross dressing'. The following description is given by J. Potter Briscoe, a prolific Nottinghamshire writer of the latter part of the 19th century. 'The vainest lady in the land could hardly take more pains in the arrangement of her attire than did some of these "Bullocks". Paints, feathers, strange clothes and other articles were brought into active requisition, and when the wearer appeared at last in the full splendour of his costume — a strange gaunt figure, with sundry tufts of feathers, and armed with a thick bludgeon — he looked the facsimile of an Indian chief in full battle array.'

In whatever part of England the celebrations took place the participants invariably disguised themselves by blackening their faces with soot, which had a horrible stinging effect on their skin. They obviously did not want to be individually accountable for their misdemeanours on Plough Monday! It was usual for them to pull either an old or a mock plough behind them which was dragged over the gardens of any misers who refused to fill their tin.

It is believed that the Plough Monday revels are the remains of fertility rites once performed on that day to celebrate the beginning of a new season's harvest and to ensure its bounty. The jumping and skipping of the Morris dancers and some of the Plough Men, and their 'changing sex' by wearing women's clothes, have definite fertility associations. The ploughing is symbolic of the next harvest season.

Many of the Nottinghamshire 'Plough Bullock Day' plays, which included a character called Tom Fool, ended with a variation of the following chorus:

> 'Good master and good mistress
> You see our fool is gone.
> We'll take it in our turn now
> To follow him along.
> We thank you for civility
> And what you've given us here
> We wish you all prosperity
> And another happy new year.'

Plough Monday often resulted in total mayhem throughout the day and drunken behaviour at night when the collecting tin was emptied. By the end of the 19th century or beginning of the 20th, most celebrations had ceased, often on the orders of the local magistrates.

The Bessie Sheppard Stone

IF you travel along the A60 almost mid way between Ravenshead and Mansfield, you will find a memorial stone standing at the southern edge of Harlow Wood. It bears an inscription to Bessie Sheppard, who was murdered on that spot in 1817.

It was on the 7th July of that year that 17 year old Bessie left her mother's house at Papplewick, south of Ravenshead, to walk into Mansfield in search of domestic work. She set out at mid-day dressed in her new shoes and carrying a light coloured cotton umbrella.

The last sighting of her was round about six o'clock when she was seen leaving Mansfield and heading for home, but the poor girl never reached her destination. The hours passed by and Mrs Sheppard's earlier annoyance at the lateness of her daughter gradually turned to a foreboding that something dreadful had happened. The night grew dark, as a search party scoured the area without results.

The young girl had left home in good spirits, optimistic of finding work at Mansfield, and there was no reason why she should go missing of her own accord. She was an uncomplicated, hard working girl with no apparent secrets. The hours dragged by until the morning, when her mother's worst fears were confirmed. Bessie's body was found lying in a ditch by the roadside, 'about 50 to 60 yards south of the third milestone.' Her skull was brutally fractured and a large hedgestake lay close to her crumpled body. The deadly instrument was later produced as evidence in court, still clotted with blood, 'and a thrill of horror ran through the spectators.'

Charles Rotherham of Sheffield, aged 33, a one-time apprentice scissors grinder turned soldier, was arrested shortly after and charged with Bessie's murder.

Rotherham had been seen drinking at the Hut Tavern close to the scene of the crime shortly after the estimated time when the act was committed. Later he slept the night at the Three Crowns inn, Redhill where he had offered Bessie's shoes and umbrella for sale. As there were no buyers he left the shoes in his bedroom when he moved on at seven o'clock the following morning. The umbrella was eventually sold at Bunny.

He was apprehended at Loughborough and taken by police escort to Nottingham where he made a full confession to the crime. At the trial the police stated that on their journey back from Leicestershire, Rotherham had been able to show them where the killing had taken place, and even took them to the hedge from which he had cut his weapon.

The soldier could not explain why he had killed the girl, whom he had never seen before that fateful day. He just struck her about the head and kept beating her until she was dead. Rotherham explained that he had gone through her pockets in search of money, but had found none. He then cut open her stays in the hope that was where she kept her cash. Her body was searched in vain and so he settled for her new shoes and umbrella, which had finally incriminated him.

A verdict of guilty was pronounced on 25th July 1817 and he was hanged at Gallows Hill, Nottingham, three days later in front of a huge jeering crowd. The Rev J. Bryan gave a long address to the onlookers who were eager for their entertainment to begin. He then prayed with the prisoner who was suitably launched into eternity, to the sound of great public rejoicing.

Rotherham's body was cut down and taken to the County Hall for the customary dissection by surgeons. When they were done the remains were put on public view in the Nisi Prius Court and eventually buried at the back of St Mary's church.

To perpetuate the memory of this tragedy some businessmen from Mansfield erected a stone on the site where the murder took place, with the following inscription:

> 'This stone was erected in memory of Elizabeth Sheppard, of Papplewick, who was murdered by Charles Rotherham, near this place, on the 7th of July, 1817, aged 17 years.'

The Boy of Nottingham

THERE is very little recorded witchcraft in Nottinghamshire, but an interesting tale is that of a young lad who was to become known as the 'Boy of Nottingham' and a charlatan exorcist named the Reverend Darrell.

At the end of the 16th century, William Somers was apprenticed to a town musician. He hated his master and his work, so he used to fake sickness in order to stay away. Somers would drink huge quantities of cold water to make his belly swell and then roll on the floor in agony. The trick worked and the artful boy added more to his repertoire and began to ape possession by devils.

His neighbours were intrigued by the youth and bought copies of the pamphlet concerning the 'Witches of Warboys' from Huntingdonshire. That case came to light in 1589 and had a familiar ring to what was happening in Nottingham. The Huntingdonshire case had attracted a lot of attention as it involved money and influence in the shape of Lady Cromwell, one of the wealthiest women in England and the grandmother of Oliver Cromwell, and Squire Throckmorton of Warboys. The apprentice's fits were similar to those of the Throckmortons' daughters and servants who were supposedly possessed by witchcraft.

William got hold of a copy, which fed his fertile imagination and he consequently claimed bewitchment 'by an old woman that he had met with, because he had not given her a hat band he had found.'

Unwittingly William Somers' life was soon to change as his conduct led him closer and closer to the influence of the Reverend John Darrell.

Darrell was a Nottinghamshire man, and had been educated at Cambridge. Upon returning to his home town, Mansfield, he became a freelance preacher. He also performed many dramatic exorcisms all over the Midlands whereby he expelled evil spirits from those who were possessed. He usually worked in front of a large crowd, who were both shocked and entertained by his incantations and the contortions of his subjects. The latter could be relied upon to throw hysterics and writhe on the ground in various stages of agony. Some would speak in strange voices and vomit up weird artefacts. It was normal for a collection to be taken at the end of the exorcism, which was money well spent to see John Darrell at work. Much of what he did was later proved to be a hoax. He was given a warning by magistrates and threatened with future imprisonment.

Then on 5th November 1597, he was invited to exorcise young Somers, but we are not told by whom.

He took William aside and explained that his case was very similar to that of Thomas Darling of Burton, whom he had exorcised in front of a great gathering. Tommy had made accusations about two women, Alice Gooderidge and her mother Elizabeth Wright, whom he alleged had bewitched him. The boy had lost his way in the woods and had behaved in an anti-social manner when he passed the two women on the pathway. Both women cursed him and this subsequently resulted in fits whereby he foamed at the mouth. Darrell reeled off many lurid descriptions of possession which he had subsequently dealt with. The case of Thomas Darling was later proved to be fraudulent.

William Somers was a willing pupil and his symptoms immediately increased at an alarming rate.

At a public meeting the next day Darrell informed the large crowd that the young boy suffered for the sins of all Nottingham. He was in fact the 'Boy of Nottingham', and bore the weight of all their misdemeanours on his young shoulders. He urged them to fast on the following day and exhorted the men to 'refrain from the company of their wives that night'. In return for their abstention they would see strange things the following day.

Two days later the exorcist preached a long sermon in front of a full congregation at St Mary's church. He listed 14 signs of possession which his student, William, innocently displayed:

'Firstly, the bewitched desire the worst food.' The boy immediately screamed out for something disgusting to eat, which was miraculously close to hand. The onlookers were reviled as he crammed it into his mouth.

'Secondly, they are unable to retain their food, are irked by continual vomiting, and are unable to digest.' William was obligingly sick and bent double with pain, moaned and howled like a sick animal.

'Thirdly, the bewitched have trouble with their heart, which feels as if torn by dogs, or eaten by serpents. . . .' William clutched himself in the region of his wicked heart.

'Fourthly, some experience frequent and sudden pains, which they cannot describe, but they shriek aloud.' The Boy of Nottingham was right on cue.

The crowd loved it and stood in silence, gasping when the actors played a particularly fine scene. The exorcist and his assistant finished their 14 turns and it was time for the exorcism to begin.

Darrell fixed his eyes firmly on Somers and laid his hand on the boy's head. Then he gave a secret command to the Devil, the Devil being the originator of the evil. Then he made a certain sign and in a loud voice began: 'As a minister of Christ and the Church and in the name of Jesus

Christ, I command you, unclean spirit, if you lie in the body of this man created by God. . . .' Finally the boy was freed from the malevolent influence and the customary collection was taken.

Cunning Darrell left room for further manipulation by stating in a very stern voice that although the boy had been delivered from all that was unholy in Nottingham, he was not free from danger. The Devil could return to him at any time in the shape of a bird, a toad, a set of dancers or even an angel. Between them they kept the pot boiling by Somers showing signs of possession at suitable intervals, and thereafter being exorcised in public in the flamboyant style expected from the freelance preacher from Mansfield.

The Boy of Nottingham's next ploy was to accuse Alice Freeman and twelve other women of causing him fits by witchcraft. They were carted off to Nottingham gaol but only two were eventually brought to trial.

Darrell condoned the boy's accusation, but Alice Freeman was the sister of an Alderman, who suspected all was not as it seemed between Darrell and Somers and had the latter taken to the House of Correction for questioning. The Boy of Nottingham confessed that his possession by the Devil had been a fraud and that he had acted under the tuition of the exorcist. This was a very serious accusation to make against a minister, and a report was made to the Archbishop of York, who set up a commission of enquiry.

Upon further examination Somers retracted his confession and went into a series of such violent fits that the enquiry believed him to be possessed.

Alice Freeman was brought to trial before Sir Edward Anderson, who had already had dealings with Darrell in the past. He urged Somers to tell the truth and William confessed again that he had been lying. The case was dismissed and a report made to the Archbishop of Canterbury.

Darrell was taken to Lambeth and examined by the

Archbishop, the Bishop of London and others. Thomas Darling, one of his earlier assistants, and William Somers both gave evidence against him and confessed that their fits and subsequent exorcisms were all fakes. They had both been taught by Darrell in the art of deception.

Darrell was stripped of his living and sent to gaol for a year where he wrote vigorous protestations of wrongful imprisonment. Many influential people continued to believe in his innocence long after his release from imprisonment, but his careers as a minister and an exorcist were both over.

However, his most permanent memorial is said to be the 72nd Canon of the Canons of London drawn up by Bishop Bancroft in 1604, which forbids any Church of England minister without prior permission by his bishop, to 'attempt upon any pretence whatever either of possession or obsession by fasting or prayer, to cast out any devil or devils, under pain of the imputation of imposture or cozenage, and deposition from the ministry.'

Bibliography

The Nottinghamshire Village Book,
Nottinghamshire Federation of Women's Institutes
Countryside Books.

Stories about the Midlands
By J. Potter Briscoe.

Old Nottingham
By J. Potter Briscoe.
Published by Hamilton, Adams & Co.

Notes About Nottingham
By C. Brown.

Nottinghamshire Facts and Fiction
By J. Potter Briscoe.

All about the Merry Tales of Gotham
By Alfred Stapleton.
Published by R. N. Pearson.

Notts and Derby Notes & Queries
Edited by J. Potter Briscoe FRHS.
Published by Frank Murray.

The Encyclopedia of Witchcraft and Demonology
By Rossell Hope Robbins.
Published by the Hamlyn Publishing Group Ltd.

Witchcraft in England
By Christina Hole.
Published by Batsford.

Highway & Byways of Nottinghamshire
By J. B. Firth.
McMillan & Co.

Food in England
By Dorothy Hartley.
Futura Publications.

The Pattern Under the Plough
By G. Ewart Evans.
Faber & Faber.

English Sports and Pastimes
By Christina Hole.
Batsford.

Robin Hood
By J. C. Holt.
Thames and Hudson.

On the Trail of Robin Hood
By Richard de Vries.
Crossbow Books.

Walkabout the Lace Market
By Doug Ritchie.
Papyrus Books.

Lord Byron
By Elizabeth Eisenberg.
J. H. Hall & Sons Ltd.

The Great Nottingham Goose Fair
By Peter Wilkes.
Trent Valley Publications.

BIBLIOGRAPHY

Then and Now
By R. Mellows.
J. & H. Bell.

A History of Nottinghamshire
By A. C. Wood.
Cooke & Vowles (1940) Ltd.

Nottinghamshire Library Scrap Books.

Memorials of Old Nottinghamshire
Edited by Everard L. Guilford, M.S.
George Allen & Company.

The White Horse of Newstead Abbey and its Rider
Reprinted from the Mansfield Reporter.

The Date Book of Nottingham 1750–1850
By John F. Sutton.

The Penny Magazine

Various press cuttings from the
Local Studies Department of
Nottinghamshire County Library.

GW00385103

Weekend Gardening

Weekend Gardening

Kathryn Bradley-Hole

Robinson
IN COLLABORATION WITH
THE DAILY TELEGRAPH

Robinson Publishing
3 The Lanchesters,
162 Fulham Palace Road,
London W6 9ER

First published by Robinson Publishing, an imprint of
Constable & Robinson Ltd, 2000

A copy of the British Library Cataloguing in Publication Data
for this title is available from the British Library

ISBN 1 84119 088 8

Edited and designed by
OutHouse Publishing Services

Illustrations by Sue Hellard

Printed and bound in Finland by WSOY

Disclaimer
The tips included throughout this book have been sent
in by readers of *The Daily Telegraph*'s Weekend section,
and they are not endorsed in any way by either the
Publishers or *The Daily Telegraph*.

Contents

Introduction

'And what do you do?' is one of those questions we are all asked at social occasions. When I reply that I'm a gardener and gardening writer, more often than not the interrogator's eyes light up and the conversation takes a swift turn into a 'Question Time' discussion. 'Now tell me, what can I do about peach-leaf curl?' 'Do grease-bands really work?' 'Why can't I grow rhubarb?' Or even, 'When will my walnut tree start to bear fruit?' Now I know why so many doctors are shy of admitting their worthy profession at parties.

But of course all gardeners love to share their knowledge and experiences, and one of the pleasures of compiling this book has been the opportunity to sift through *The Daily Telegraph* readers' own tips and wrinkles. Some of the many imaginative suggestions for making the gardener's life easier are included in this book.

One question I'm often asked is, 'What plant can I buy for someone called Betty? Or William? Or Rosina, or whoever? In answer, I have compiled what I believe to be the most comprehensive guide to the cultivars bearing people's names yet published. Over 700 names are listed.

I hope these 'extras' that you won't find in other gardening books will prove as valuable and fascinating to you as they have done to me, and that the month-by-month guide to work in the garden will be a continuously useful *aide memoire*.

Suggesting gardening tasks for any particular week of the year is always fraught with difficulty.

The mild south-west can enjoy golden sheets of daffodils and breathtaking blooms on magnolias in February when central and northern regions are still enveloped in blizzards, with ground so cold and hard that bulbs and blossoms wait six more weeks before braving the elements. We therefore decided to group practical work under broader, monthly headings; in extreme areas, your local conditions will dictate whether to do a particular job, such as seed-sowing, early or late in the suggested month, or even to delay it until the start of the next one. Generally, though, the monthly format will suit nearly everyone.

The 'Looking Good Now' sections in each month highlight the plants that I think are the most rewarding at that particular time of the year. And for each season, I have selected a topical subject for more detailed discussion: natural pest control; container gardening; topiary; and gardening in harmony with wildlife. Wherever possible, I have included names of the stockists of the plants and equipment mentioned in text. But if you have any difficulty finding a particular plant, consult a copy of *The RHS Plant Finder* (published by Dorling Kindersley in book format or CD Rom) the annually updated directory of who is growing what in nurseries around Britain.

Lastly, I have many people to thank for their help in writing this book: my colleagues at *The Daily Telegraph* and Robinson Publishing; talented illustrator Sue Hellard for her delightful drawings, and of course *The Daily Telegraph*'s readers, with whom I am honoured and delighted to share gardening advice, anecdotes and correspondence. Thank you.

Kathryn Bradley-Hole

January

Midwinter means different things to different people. Much depends on where you live and the harshness of the season. Some of us will experience plenty of frosts, which can be devastating for tender plants if they are not sufficiently protected, but frosts also yield benefits. A really cold snap in winter helps to clear the garden of prevailing insect pests, and the penetration of frost into hard ground helps to break it down and make it easier to work when the warmer weather returns.

When the season is mild, the viburnums and winter cherries produce more blooms and, at times, the month of January can look deceptively like a brief dress rehearsal for spring.

ORNAMENTAL GARDEN

Pruning & Planting

Wisteria

One of the first jobs of the new year is to give wisteria its winter pruning. Cut back last year's whippy stems to just two or three buds at the base of each. These will provide the flowering spurs for this year's blossoms. For the trained standard (mop-head) wisterias, aim to develop a rounded head as you prune; if the head on mature specimens is congested, carefully remove some older wood.

Roses

Plant new roses, but stay off the soil if it is sticky, wet or frozen. Bare-rooted bushes waiting to be planted should be 'heeled-in' (laid on their sides with the roots covered by soil in a shallow trench) until they can be planted.

New shrubs

When the weather is fine, continue planting dormant, deciduous shrubs and hedges.

Take hardwood cuttings of the dogwoods that have colourful winter twigs (*Cornus alba* and *C. stolonifera* types). Insert 8–10 inch ((20–25cm) long cuttings to half their depth in an open area of ground, where you can leave them undisturbed until next autumn when they will have rooted.

Hellebores

To see the flowers of the many Lenten hellebores (*Helleborus orientalis*) at their most glorious in the coming weeks, cut away last year's tattered leaves now. The same goes for *H. niger*, the white-petalled Christmas rose. And if you intend bringing some cut stems indoors, protect selected plants with cloches to maintain perfect blooms.

No need to cut away leaves of *H. foetidus* or the robust *H. argutifolius* unless they are unusually scruffy, but their tall stems, laden with pale-green blooms, may need discreet staking with canes if plants have become overgrown and lax. This is also a good time to buy container-grown hellebores that are starting to flower.

Biennials

Check that spring biennials, such as wallflowers, sweet williams and polyanthus, are well bedded-in and haven't lifted during cold weather.

Mulches

Provided the weather is mild, finish laying manure and compost mulches on flower borders as soon as possible. The job becomes more difficult when spring growth starts pushing through the ground.

Frost Protection

Camellias

When frosty weather is forecast, throw a blanket of horticultural fleece over vulnerable camellias to give the flowerbuds some protection.

❋ ***Quick Tip*** ❋

For simpler gardening, try using a paint-scraper – it replaces trowel, hand-fork, hoe, and chopper. *Mrs S Butcher*

Birds
Ensure that bird-feeders are regularly replenished, and that there is clean (unfrozen) water for birds to drink. Hang up nesting boxes, and the birds will help deal with your garden pests in the coming year.

Ponds
If there are fish in the pond, check that the water is not completely frozen over during cold snaps. If ice forms a solid layer, toxic gases lethal to fish can build up underneath it. To create an air-hole, stand a pan of boiling water on the surface so that it slowly melts the ice underneath; never smash the ice to break it open. Placing a floating ball in the pond before it freezes over will keep one small area ice-free; you can then pour hot water over the ball to open up the hole.

Paths & Lawns

Avoid ruining sodden grass and garden soil underfoot by making a temporary pathway to walk on when you work. Scaffold boards from builders' merchants are useful, but here's a really good idea: the Portapath from Agriframes (tel. 01342 310000) is a lightweight polypropylene interlocking path that clips together like caterpillar tracks and can be hosed-down and rolled up after use.

Mowers
If you haven't already sent the mower for cleaning and servicing, now is a good time to do so. Repair shops get very busy in spring when everyone else seems to want their machinery serviced.

Moss
Choose a mild day to clean moss and algae from slippery paths, using a stiff brush and paving cleaner. Scrape out weeds from between paving stones.

Mail Orders

As catalogues for young (seedling and plug-) plants begin to arrive, it is tempting to place your order straight away; but some suppliers despatch feeble, tiny plants much too early, making their survival unlikely without specialist equipment. If you want to place an early order, ask for a despatch date, and request a late-spring delivery if necessary.

KITCHEN GARDEN

Soil Warming & Digging

Select a sunny part of the vegetable garden to warm up now. Cover it with clear (not black), firmly anchored polythene sheeting or cloches.

❃ *Quick Tips* ❃

Use chicken-feed to melt ice on paths – it doesn't damage plants as salt does, and the birds will eat it once the ice has thawed. *Rajiv Bobal*

To eradicate moles from lawns, scoop small trowels of used cat-litter into and under the mounds. *Vivienne S Tennant*

With the covered soil partially dried and sheltered from cold winds, it will be ready for some early sowings next month.

If you use a 'dig', as opposed to a 'no-dig' (raised bed) method of raising crops, continue digging over heavy ground whenever the soil is not too wet. Frost will then help to break down the large clod, making the soil more workable in spring. Remove roots of perennial weeds as you go.

Vegetables

Check stored root vegetables, onions and fruit and discard any showing signs of rot.

Onions

Order onion sets (baby onions) for planting out in March. Unpack the bags as soon as they are arrive, and lay sets out somewhere dry and frost-free until planting time.

Garlic

Garlic grows best when it has endured some winter chill and spring rains, so plant out individual cloves in a sunny spot now: pointed end up, 6 or 7 inches (15cm) apart, with 1 inch (2.5cm) of soil covering the tip. (On heavy or wet soils, start off cloves in modules or small pots of soil-based potting compost and leave in a sheltered place outdoors, ready to plant out in spring.)

Vines

Grape-vines (including ornamentals such as *Vitis coignetiae*) need pruning now. If left until late winter, the rising sap will bleed from every cut. Prune back last year's stems to one or two buds.

New Seeds

If you fancy growing something a bit different this year, have a look through the mail-order seed catalogues, which offer much more choice than any garden centre does. One of my current favourites is the *Ferme de Sainte Marthe* catalogue (tel. 01932 266630, fax 01932 252707) from France, now offered in an English edition. It features very wide ranges of tomatoes, pumpkins, squashes and gourds (including loofahs, so you can grow your own bath sponges!), salads, chilli-peppers, and old vegetable varieties, all from certified organic stock.

INDOORS & UNDER GLASS

Indoor Plants

Put flowering pot-plants, such as African violet and flaming Katy (*Kalanchoe*), beside bright windows so that they can take advantage of maximum light levels; but don't trap them in the cold behind curtains at night.

Seeds & Cuttings

Sow salads

For the earliest radish and lettuce crops, sow some towards the end of this month, in gentle heat in the greenhouse, in pots or grow-bags, but expect germination to be fairly slow at this time of year.

❋ *Quick Tip* ❋

Save Christmas holly decorations. When dry, place in your vegetable and flower borders to deter cats. *W A Kennett*

Indoor potatoes
Start off the earliest seed-potatoes on the bench of a heated greenhouse or on a frost-free windowsill to get sturdy short shoots or 'chits'. Chitted 'Swift' and 'Dunluce' (from Marshalls Seeds, tel. 01945 466711) can be pot-forced from now in a frost-free greenhouse or conservatory for a really early crop. Plant them singly into 12-inch (30cm) pots.

Potting On

Pot on rooted cuttings of shrubs, woody herbs and pelargoniums into soil-based John Innes No.2 potting compost. Plants grown in this compost transplant much more easily into the open ground than those raised in soil-less compost.

Pest Check

Inspect foliage of overwintering plants and emerging bulbs in the greenhouse for signs of aphids. Small colonies can be rubbed away with fingers and thumb.

Cleaning

Glass
To maximise the available daylight, clean greenhouse and conservatory glass both inside and out. Cleaning also helps to remove overwintering pests and their eggs. If you have put up greenhouse insulation, check that it is still in place, and not letting in cold draughts.

Pots
Clean any pots and seed-trays that were stored unwashed – a tedious job, but better done now than the moment you need to use them in spring.

Quick Tip

To rid your property of seagulls and pigeons, put up a plastic owl. *Stella Walton*

Use a solution of bleach or household disinfectant to clean off lurking bacteria that may cause disease, and rinse thoroughly.

QUESTIONS & ANSWERS

Cut flowers and foliage are quite expensive at this time of year. Any ideas for winter plants that I can grow to cut and bring indoors in future would be welcome.

Jean Harris, Winchester

For winter foliage, grow one or two evergreen shrubs that you don't mind stealing the odd branch from. Eucalyptus, variegated holly, and gold-splashed *Elaeagnus pungens* 'Maculata' are all very attractive. If your garden is sheltered, you might also try growing some variegated myrtle.

For fragrant flowers, you could plant winter honeysuckle (*Lonicera fragrantissima*), and wintersweet (*Chimonanthus praecox*). And small vases filled with Algerian iris (*Iris unguicularis*) and delicate snowdrops are particularly delightful in midwinter.

ꟈ

Where does the saying 'Rosemary for remembrance' come from? And will growing the herb improve my memory?
R Barker, Penrith

In Shakespeare's *Hamlet* (IV, v), Ophelia says, 'There's rosemary, that's for remembrance'. The herb has a very long history of usefulness. Since ancient times it has been used in medicine, and as an ingredient in incense because of its strong, penetrating scent. Its essential oil has a stimulating effect on the central nervous system and its fragrance is known to induce feelings of mental clarity.

ꟈ

I have brought some pots of geraniums (pelargoniums) indoors for the winter. They are in a sunny spot beside the patio doors, and have continued to grow, but are looking straggly and leggy. Can I cut them back now?
E Anderson, Cambridge

These sound like the popular zonal pelargoniums and, yes, you can cut them back to a more manageable size, but don't strip them completely bare of their leaves. Give them a little water and a weak liquid feed and they will send out shoots further down to produce bushier plants. Don't throw away the pruned-off pieces; put 3-4 inch (7–10cm) long cuttings into pots of proprietary seed/cutting compost near a window in a warm room. Water sparingly, keeping the compost just on the dry side.

Looking Good in January ...

Witch hazel

Witch hazel – a native of North America and the Far East – is more than just an item in the medicine cabinet; it happens to be one of the most stunning winter plants. The most attractive varieties come from China, but it grows beautifully in our own gardens, too. The Chinese witch hazel, *Hamamelis mollis*, has large, spidery flowers of brilliant golden yellow, clustered along bare, spreading branches. It eventually grows to about 8 feet (2.5m) high and wide. A few stems cut for the house bring vibrant colour and a light, sweet fragrance into the home. Grow it in an open position in good, fertile, well-drained soil that doesn't dry out in summer. Be sure to give it an autumn mulch of well-rotted leaf-mould or compost.

Corkscrew hazel

With its wiggly stems twisting themselves into delightful squiggles, the corkscrew hazel, *Corylus avellana* 'Contorta', is one of nature's eccentrics, and understandably popular with flower-arrangers. Because of all its changes of direction during growth, it forms a dense shrub, eventually attaining around 10 feet (3m) in height. Discovered in the Gloucestershire hedgerows around 1863, it's also known as Harry Lauder's Walking Stick, after the legendary Scottish music-hall comedian.

Winter is its time of glory, when yellow tassels of pollen-carrying catkins dangle from bare stems. It's easy to grow, as it's not fussy about soil, but if it is not to become a tangled mess it should be pruned back to a few main stems every couple of years. And I would suggest giving it a not-too-prominent position because its contorted leaves are much less attractive than the bare winter stems!

February

This can be a bewitching, unpredictable month, with gales, snow and torrents of rain – and then, occasionally, a few fugitive days of sunshine that put you more in mind of May. Early bulbs, such as crocuses and the reticulata types of iris, combine with snowdrops and winter aconites to set the gardening pulse racing once more, and most welcome they are, too, after the gloom of winter. Perhaps it comes as a surprise that some trees and shrubs will choose this moment to give their best show. They are, of course, competing for the attentions of the relatively few pollinating insects at large at this time of year. Many of them therefore offer the bonus attraction of sweet scent among their flowers.

ORNAMENTAL GARDEN

Winter Cheer

If parts of the garden look dull at this time of year, consider how they could be beefed up with a few choice evergreens. Variegated yuccas bring lively foliage colours and spiky form into borders. Many camellias, and fragrant-flowered *Choisya ternata* have very shiny, light-reflective foliage. Evergreen euphorbias such as *E. wulfenii* and *E. nicaeensis* make characterful grey-green clumps, poised ready for their spring flowering.

Planting & Potting

Cyclamen

Dainty outdoor cyclamen, with their quaintly marbled leaves, are easiest to establish in the garden if planted while they are actively growing, rather than as dormant bulbs. Hardy *Cyclamen coum*, now in bloom, is widely available at garden centres at about this time, and *C. libanoticum* is suitable for mild positions. Plant them into humus-rich but freely draining soil, in areas of semi-shade.

New bulbs

Plant up empty pots and window-boxes with cheerful primulas and emerging spring bulbs.

New lilies

Pot up lily bulbs, three per 10–12 inch (25–30cm) pot. John Innes No.2 or No.3 potting compost is ideal, being loamy and free-draining but heavy enough to give pots stability. Put some crocks or grit in the bottom for added drainage and plant bulbs quite deeply – with around 4 inches (10cm) of soil covering the tops. For a crisp finish, and to prevent weed and moss growth, cover the soil surface with a thin layer of horticultural grit.

The popular Asiatic hybrid lilies make good pot-plants, although their large, upward-facing flowers are too gaudy for some tastes. More demure are species lilies and 'Turk's-cap' types, with reflexed petals resembling a turban. Look out for *Lilium tenuifolium pumilum*, a dainty plant (20 inches/50cm tall) with brilliant-scarlet 'turbans'; 'Citronella Strain' is a good yellow, and dramatic 'Black Beauty' has swept-back crimson petals finely margined with white. (They are available from bulb specialists, including Bloms, tel. 01234 709099).

Repairs & Maintenance

Timber repairs

Repair fences, trelliswork and pergola timbers now, before plants are actively growing again.

Plant labels

Now is a good time to sort out plant labels – a nice indoor job when the weather is foul. Garish plastic nursery labels can be replaced with something more discreet, such as black, scratch-on labels (sold by MacPenny's, tel. 01425 672348). I find it difficult to scratch a name neatly onto the label with the metal scriber, so I use a silver-gel pen instead.

❋ *Quick Tip* ❋

If you like mussels, save the shells to 'crock' your pots. *David Cane*

Clearing up
Start the spring tidy-up by removing the remains of last year's annuals if they were kept through winter. Clear any decaying foliage to the compost heap. Gently use a fork or narrow rake to turn over the soil surface in flower and shrub borders, mixing in well rotted compost and slow-release fertiliser as you go, and run a hoe through gravel paths and mulches to dislodge weed seedlings.

Weather-Watch

Continue monitoring weather conditions. Stay off the soil and grass if it's very wet. Protect vulnerable plants from sudden cold spells, by covering them with horticultural fleece.

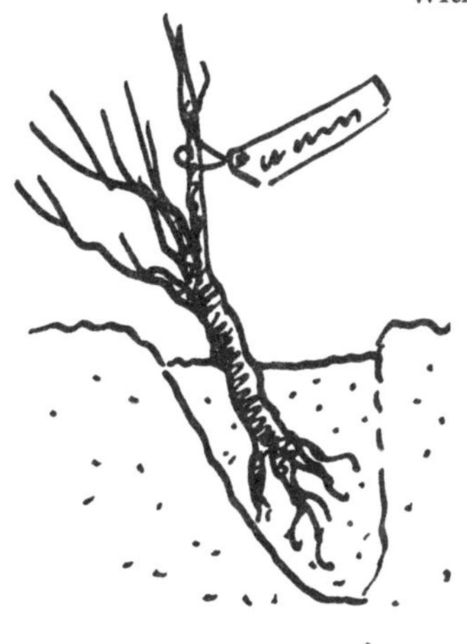

Bare-rooted plants
If the ground is too wet to finish planting trees, hedges and shrubs, heel-in bare-rooted stock on an unused piece of ground until the weather improves. Dig a small trench with one sloping side. Put the rootball in the trench, laying the plant on its side, and cover over the roots with the excavated soil.

Pests & Diseases

Slug-traps
Put out slug-baits and traps to prevent damage to early-flowering herbaceous plants.

Wood disease

Check woody plants for signs of coral-spot fungus, which is easy to see while plants are still leafless. Cut out and burn all branches showing a rash of orange, spotty pustules. These branches are already dead, but use clean secateurs to cut back to healthy wood, and disinfect your tools after use.

KITCHEN GARDEN

Soil & Compost

Apply a light dressing of lime or calcified seaweed (which contains other trace nutrients) to kitchen garden soil, especially where leafy vegetables such as brassicas will be grown.

Turn compost heaps now, while they are relatively wet, and cover over with sections of old carpet or other material to help maintain the heat.

Pruning & Planting

Garlic

If you didn't plant out your garlic last month, do it now. If the ground is too wet, push cloves into outdoor pots of gritty soil for planting out later.

Early spuds

Late this month, in mild areas, plant out potatoes that have chitted (sprouted) in recent weeks. Planted closely, (about 1 foot/30cm apart each way) and 5–6 inches (12–15cm) deep, they will produce an abundant harvest of small new potatoes. Cover with protective spun-polypropylene fabric (such as Envirofleece Winterweight, from garden centres or from Agralan, tel. 01285 86001).

Unusual vegetables
Unlike globe artichokes, Jerusalem artichokes have edible root-tubers. They are easy to grow, and make reliable wind-breakers (in more than one sense, as anyone who has eaten them will know). Plant the tubers now, in rows in well-manured soil, 4–6 inches (10–15cm) deep, 18 inches (45cm) apart. Plant them vertically, with the scarred end (where the tuber was cut) facing downwards. Water regularly in dry spells, and remove flower-buds as they form to retain energy in the roots. Interestingly, Jerusalem artichokes have nothing to do with the Holy City (they come from North America); their name derives from *girasole*, Italian for sunflower, to which they are closely related.

Fruit trees
Finish winter pruning of apple and pear trees.

INDOORS & UNDER GLASS

Ensure cold frames and greenhouses are adequately ventilated during the day, but remember to close them again when temperatures drop in the afternoon.

❋ *Quick Tips* ❋

To remove barbecue grease stains from a patio, cover with cat-litter, grind with your heel, leave for several hours, then just sweep up. *M Groom*

Fine bran and eggshells (oven-dried and crushed) sprinkled around vulnerable plants deters slugs and snails without harming birds. *Mrs R Pettit*

Seeds, Bulbs & Tubers

Check you have adequate supplies of seed or cell-trays, pots, labels and sowing compost before starting a pleasant day's sowing. Also check supplies of fine sand, grit and vermiculite if you use them. It's infuriating to have to stop work to make an urgent shopping trip for these things.

Carefully prick out seedlings as soon as they are large enough to handle, holding them by the seed-leaves, never by the stems.

Hyacinths

Put emerging hyacinth bulbs into the brightest possible position to stimulate flowering. Give pots a quarter-turn daily to encourage the new leaves to grow straight and upright.

Dahlias

Named dahlia hybrids do not come true from seed, but you can increase stocks of favourite ones by forcing new shoots to provide cuttings. Submerge the tubers in pots or seed-trays filled with damp potting compost (add some grit to improve aeration and drainage). Remove to a bright, warm place, keep the soil slightly damp, and take 3–4 inch (7–10cm) cuttings from the shoots that develop in the coming weeks.

Sow seeds of bedding dahlias in trays of loam-based (John Innes) seed-compost. Keep in a propagator set at 65°F (18°C) and, when the seedlings

❋ *Quick Tip* ❋

Old tennis balls placed on the tops of canes make effective eye-protectors. *Mrs J Cross*

are large enough to handle, prick them out into cell-trays or small pots. Pretty varieties include the 'Sangria' strain (Unwins, tel. 01945 588522), which has semi-double flowers in a broad range of colours, 'Collarette Dandy', which has festive, contrasting inner and outer petals, and the demure, single-flowered 'Heirloom Border Species' (both from Thompson & Morgan, tel. 01473 690869).

New begonias

Start off begonia tubers in a heated greenhouse or propagator, kept at a constant temperature of 55–64°F (13–18°C). Push the tubers into seed-trays filled with moistened coir or other loamless compost, with the hollow side uppermost. Once the leafy shoots emerge the tubers can be potted on individually into 4–5 inch (10–13cm) pots.

New vegetables
For early crops of carrots, broad beans, tomatoes, cucumbers, and early salads, sow the seeds in a warm greenhouse now.

Artichokes
Globe artichokes are enormously decorative, and not difficult to grow from seed if sown now, two seeds per 3-inch (8cm) pot, and germinated at 65°F (18°C); remove the weakest seedling that develops in each case. Set out young plants in late April, either in the kitchen garden or in flower borders, to make for a bold summer display when mature.

Indoor cyclamen
Check greenhouse cyclamen for signs of moulding leaves, and remove any bad bits carefully. Place a quarter-inch (60mm) layer of clean horticultural grit over the soil surface to keep leaves

❃ Quick Tip ❃

An old ironing table makes an excellent height-adjustable potting table in the garden or greenhouse, and it needs very little storage space.
V C Jones

Tickets £1 each

Viva! 141243

Spring FUNDRAISING RAFFLE

1st Prize – £2000

2nd Prize – £300

3rd Prize – £200

Fourth and Fifth prizes: fab *Viva!* hampers

PLUS Two runners-up prizes: £50 vouchers from Vegetarian Shoes

Contact raffle promoter
Jeremy Ludlow for details
Tel: 0117 970 4634
Email: jeremy@viva.org.uk
Draw date: 11 June 2018

Return ticket stub by 4 June 2018

VEGETARIAN SHOES

www.viva.org.uk
Viva!, 8 York Court, Wilder Street,
Bristol BS2 8QH
Charity no. 1037486

Viva! 141242

Spring

FUNDRAISING RAFFLE

Tickets £1 each

1st Prize – £2000

2nd Prize – £300

3rd Prize – £200

Fourth and Fifth prizes: fab *Viva!* hampers

PLUS Two runners-up prizes: £50 vouchers from Vegetarian Shoes

Contact raffle promoter Jeremy Ludlow for details
Tel: 0117 970 4634
Email: jeremy@viva.org.uk
Draw date: 11 June 2018

Return ticket stub by 4 June 2018

VEGETARIAN SHOES

www.viva.org.uk
Viva!, 8 York Court, Wilder Street,
Bristol BS2 8QH
Charity no. 1037486

Viva! 141241

Spring FUNDRAISING RAFFLE

Tickets £1 each

1st Prize – £2000

2nd Prize – £300

3rd Prize – £200

Fourth and Fifth prizes: fab *Viva!* hampers

PLUS Two runners-up prizes: £50 vouchers from Vegetarian Shoes

Contact raffle promoter
Jeremy Ludlow for details
Tel: 0117 970 4634
Email: jeremy@viva.org.uk
Draw date: 11 June 2018

Return ticket stub by 4 June 2018

VEGETARIAN SHOES

www.viva.org.uk
Viva!, 8 York Court, Wilder Street,
Bristol BS2 8QH
Charity no. 1037486

and stems away from damp soil, and remember to water them only from the bottom to avoid having water rotting the crown.

Pruning

Prune zonal pelargoniums that have become leggy indoors. Follow with a light watering and weak liquid feed, and keep plants in a bright position to encourage new growth. There are many good new pelargoniums (zonal, scented and cascading/ivy-leaved types) available as plug-plants from various seed companies. Order now to beat the March deadlines for plants to be sent by post.

Houseplants

Mist houseplants with a fine spray of water to counteract the drying effects of central heating.

Pests

Vine-weevils

Check the rootballs of overwintered greenhouse plants for vine-weevil grubs. Succulents, fuchsias, *Primula auricula* and other primulas are especially vulnerable to these destructive root-feeding pests. At this time of year the most effective method of destroying them is to crush visible grubs and dispose of all the soil around plant roots; replant into brand-new potting compost. Or, if the infestation is serious, water in Bio Provado vine-weevil killer, which eradicates both grubs and eggs.

Fly-traps

Remove all old sticky yellow fly-traps, and hang up new ones suspending them just above the tops of plants on the greenhouse bench.

QUESTIONS & ANSWERS

A friend recently offered to buy me some trees as a 'garden-warming' present, and I've decided on apple trees. I live in Yorkshire, which suffers hard winters, and I wondered if any varieties were particularly suited to my area?

D Metcalf, York

You're right in thinking that some varieties of fruit tree are better suited to your local climate than others. This is not just because of the cold winters but because spring comes so late that blossoms can easily be ruined by late frosts.

'Brownlees Russet', 'Epicure' and 'Balsam' are all excellent and are said to do very well in your region. If you'd rather buy old varieties, 'Improved Cockpit' and 'Court Pendu Plat' also do very well in the north. It is worth going to a local specialist for the trees, as the stock will be particularly appropriate – R.V. Roger Nurseries in Pickering (tel. 01751 472226) has a large selection of fruit trees. And, remember, to get good crops you need compatible trees, which flower at the same time, for cross-pollination. Ask the nursery for advice.

I bought some ornamental gourds from a florist last year, but would like to grow my own this year if it is possible to do so. Some advice would be welcome.

Jean Turner, Winchester

Gourds make unusual and effective indoor decorations, and they are easy to grow. Seeds can be started off in pots indoors in late April, or sown

directly outdoors in late May. Choose a sunny spot in ordinary, free-draining soil, and provide a supporting wigwam of canes, or an archway or trelliswork for the climbing stems. Water and mulch generously and harvest the attractive, knobbly fruits in autumn. Seeds of colourful mixed varieties are available from Thompson & Morgan (tel. 01473 688821) but, as far as I know, the widest selection currently available is from Ferme de Sainte Marthe (tel. 01932 26660).

ꟺ

There is a fairly large magnolia in our front garden, which we like very much, especially when it flowers in spring. The trouble is, it does block out some of the light from our house. I have been thinking of moving it to the back garden. Is this a good idea, and when should it be done?

C Clark, Burgess Hill

Magnolias, particularly *M.* x *soulangeana*, are so stunning when in bloom that they are often planted as front garden specimens; but people don't realise how large they can grow, and it is virtually impossible to transplant them (as I have learned through bitter experience). They hate root disturbance, and seldom recover from it. I can only recommend some judicious pruning, in mid-to-late July, to open up the canopy and let in more light – but be careful not to destroy its shape.

Looking Good in February ...

Crocus tommasinianus

There can be sleet, snow, frost or rain, but this early-flowering species crocus takes it all in its stride. The lavender-coloured flowers are slender and graceful, paler at the centre, with a contrasting bunch of egg-yolk yellow stamens. Its willingness to self-sow means that a handful of bulbs will rapidly become a sea of soft violet. Full sun is best, but partial shade will suit, too, and it's unfussy about soil. It dies away rapidly after flowering, so it's a good choice for planting in turf, as you won't need to wait too long before you can mow the area.

Japanese apricot

Anticipating the parade of blossoms that its relations, the flowering cherries, will put on in a few weeks' time, the slender-stemmed Japanese apricot, *Prunus mume* 'Beni-chidori' likes to be ahead of the game. And for late winter blossoms, it is without equal.

Grow it in a sheltered, bright position and you can rely on this small tree to put on a stunning display of raspberry-pink blooms. It is compact enough to be fitted into small gardens, for it take years to achieve its ultimate height and spread of 10 feet (3m). And with a carpet of yellow aconites, some *Galanthus* 'S. Arnott' snowdrops, and vivid-lilac *Crocus tommasinianus* around its feet, you will have a late-winter picture as heart-warming as toasted mallows over a log fire.

March

The start of spring is a joyous thing to behold as countless bulbs push their noses above the bare earth while late-winter's blossoms still cling to bare stems. The rich blues, mauves and golden yellows that predominate at this time of year with the blossoming of the crocuses, scillas and daffodils have a clean freshness that encapsulates the character of the season. The freshness of the air is palpable, too, but sometimes so sharp that it's useful to have a greenhouse – the ideal retreat – where you can potter among your plants and flowers, whose perfume – hanging sweetly in the air for it has nowhere else to go – will soothe the nostrils as you busy yourself with potting, sowing and planning.

ORNAMENTAL GARDEN

Roses

If you haven't already pruned your bush-roses (hybrid teas and floribundas), do so now. Using clean, sharp secateurs, remove all dead, damaged or diseased stems, and cut away the thin, spindly twigs. Remember that hard pruning encourages strong growth, so cut back weak shoots hard, cutting above an outward-facing bud and leaving about an inch (2.5cm) of last year's growth. On stronger stems, leave about 2–3 inches (5–7.5cm) of last year's growth.

Shrub-roses require less radical pruning. Using a pruning saw, take out about one third of the oldest and thickest branches at their base. Tidy up the remaining stems by using your secateurs to trim the top of the shrub, reducing the stems' height by about 4 inches (10cm).

Trees and Shrubs

March is the time to hard-prune late-flowering shrubs such as caryopteris, *Buddleia davidii*,

leycesteria and lavatera. However, if you live in a cold area that is still subject to regular frosts, you should delay pruning for another three to four weeks.

At the end of this month, lightly prune mop-head and lace-cap hydrangeas. Take off the old flowerheads if you kept them over the winter (cutting each stem above a strong pair of buds), and completely remove any spindly twigs. On old, congested bushes, take out some of the oldest stems at ground level. *Hydrangea paniculata* and its cultivars (such as 'Kyushu' and 'Grandiflora') flower best when given harsher treatment: hard-prune them, leaving just two or three pairs of buds low down on each branch.

The popular, silver-leaved pear tree *Pyrus salicifolia* 'Pendula' has wiry, weeping branches that tangle into a bird's nest if left unpruned. You can take advantage of this habit and trim it after its April flowering into a dense, topiarised 'mophead'. I prefer to prune now – before the leaves have expanded – because the job is more difficult later on. I thin out the head into a light, filigree umbrella, which enhances the tree's resemblance to an olive tree. (Mediterranean plants, such as alliums, irises, lavenders and sage, therefore look good in its company). You do lose a lot of the flowers by pruning this way, but since the flowers are a rather dirty white I am

❋ ***Quick Tip*** ❋

Use a broken garden fork or blunt spade stuck in the ground by the door as a boot-scraper. *Jack Leaman*

prepared to lose them for the sake of the tree's overall appearance.

Hostas
This is a good time to dig out and divide large clumps of hostas – before the leaves are expanding. Use a spade to slice through the solid rootball, cutting it like a cake into several sections, each with some shoots at the top. Replant some of the smaller pieces at the original level.

Lawns

We're back into the grass-growing season, but at this time of year the mower's blades should still be set high.

Soil

It isn't too late to improve heavy clay soils and so create better planting conditions for the season ahead, but you need to act quickly. Dig plenty of coarse grit (3–5mm-sized stones) into the top 18 inches (45cm) of soil over the whole of the area to be improved: for every 3–4 square yards (2.5–3.5 sq m) of soil, incorporate one large wheelbarrow-load of grit

KITCHEN GARDEN

Fruits

Provide wall-trained outdoor apricots, peaches and cherries with fleece or polythene protection to save their buds from frost damage. There are few visiting insects at this time of year, so, to assist flower pollination, transfer pollen from one open blossom to another with a soft paintbrush.

Seeds

Herbs
Lift, divide and replant clumps of chives in a sunny position. Sow chervil, fennel, dill and parsley outdoors.

Broad beans
Sow broad beans in double rows or blocks outdoors, spacing them 8–9 inches (20–23cm) apart, 1½ inches (4 cm) deep. (Organically grown seed of early yielding 'Futura' is available from Chase Organics, tel. 01932 253666).

Weeding

Pull out weeds emerging around fruit trees, soft-fruit bushes and strawberry plants to prevent them competing for nutrients.

Slugs & Snails

Slugs and snails thrive at this time of year, feasting on the numerous soft, young shoots that are appearing everywhere. They are especially

prevalent when the season is mild and wet. To trap them, simply scatter spare roofing tiles or pot-crocks over your flowerbeds. Slugs and snails will use them as hiding places, making it easy for you to locate the pests and destroy them each morning.

INDOORS & UNDER GLASS

Prepare for the growing season by cleaning all greenhouse windows and cold-frames to ensure that seedlings receive maximum light. Also, of course, windows indoors should be cleaned wherever plants are being grown.

Buy growing bags now if you use them, and lay them in the greenhouse for several days to allow the compost to warm up before you start sowing.

Vegetables

Root crops
Sow root crops under glass in modular trays rather than in open seed-trays. This will help to reduce root disturbance when you come to pot them on.

Tomatoes
Seeds of outdoor tomatoes must be sown now. Sow indoors, in pots of soilless compost, for planting out after the risk of frost has passed. Huge

❋ *Quick Tips* ❋

You can sow seeds singly by using the dampened end of a matchstick. *Major H B Gray*

A lit candle left in an unheated (but lined) greenhouse will be enough to keep the frost off. *Rita Fitzmaurice*

ranges of tomato seed, including yellow, pointed, striped, calabash (gourd-like), green, cherry, pear, pepper and plum types are offered by Simpson's Seeds (tel. 01883 715242). Organic composts to grow them in are sold by Chase Organics (tel. 01932 253666).

Young seedlings
If you have sown seeds recently, don't forget to separate (prick out) the seedlings and pot them up carefully as soon as they are large enough to handle. Overcrowded seedlings rapidly become leggy and weak, resulting in inferior plants.

Cacti

Windowsill cacti often look bedraggled at winter's end, but they quickly recover when set in fresh soil. Use proprietary cactus compost, which is very free draining, and pot on into a slightly larger pot. To avoid piercing your hands on the spines, wrap a strip of folded newspaper or card around the plant to make a 'handle' by which you can lift the plant safely. Water sparingly around the edge of the pot to avoid wetting the plant.

Whitefly

Inspect the sticky, yellow fly-traps that you hung up close to greenhouse plants a couple of weeks ago. The number of whiteflies on the paper will indicate the extent of the infestation. The tiny *Encarsia* parasitic wasp effectively controls whitefly under glass from mid-spring, or when an average temperature of 50°F (10°C) can be maintained. (*See* Natural Pest Control, pages 44–5).

QUESTIONS & ANSWERS

Last summer, I admired a beautiful white poppy that was as tall as me. I was told it was a Californinan variety. Can you give me the proper name and suggest where I could buy it?

Caroline Whitaker, London

The poppy you saw, I'm certain, was *Romneya coulteri* – a tall, shrubby plant, with large, white, papery petals and bright-yellow central stamens that give it a flamboyant 'fried-egg' appearance. It likes a very sunny position, and needs light, free-draining soil. It can take a while to get established. If you are unable to obtain it locally, you can mail-order it from Abbotsbury Sub-Tropical Gardens (tel. 01305 871344), or Hopleys Plants (tel. 01279 842509). Note that the latter supplies plants during October and November only.

ꟼ

My mother is getting on in years, but still enjoys her small garden. I wonder if there are any ways in which we could make the garden easier for her to tend?

A J Brand, Wolverhampton

If your mother has a lawn, and wants to keep it, make sure it is of a simple shape, without awkward cut-out bits for beds. This will cut down on time spent mowing and edging, which are the most regularly time-consuming chores throughout much of the year.

You can reduce the workload further by filling the flowerbeds with plenty of shrubs. For year-round interest, choose some evergreens, such as mahonias, variegated hollies and elaeagnus for winter foliage and berries, and some flowering shrubs, such as spiraeas, hebes, hydrangeas and hibiscus. These, along with plenty of bulbs in the ground, will make for year-round variety and

❃ *Quick Tips* ❃

Don't buy plants straight after a very cold spell. Their roots may have been badly affected, even if the stems look healthy. *Mrs J Currie*

When planning a new outline for a lawn, use a hosepipe to form a 'template, and then view the overall effect from an upstairs window, before you start digging. *S Anthony*

For the first lawn cut of the season, use an old blade in the mower so that any stones that may have found their way into the grassr don't ruin a new blade. *D Lloyd*

colour in the garden while demanding very little maintenance.

You could also build some raised beds, as these allow easy access for planting and maintenance but without the need to bend down to ground level. Good-quality, lightweight tools can also help to ease the strain of gardening, and a pair of ratchet secateurs makes pruning much easier for anyone without much strength in their hands.

℘

The forsythia in my front garden is very dull except when it flowers briefly in spring. Can I liven it up by planting something to climb through it for later colour?

Len Hall, Bridport

You could train a not-too-overbearing rose, such as 'Pink Perpétué', or the climbing, white-flowered 'Iceberg', through it. Alternatively, you could use climbing annuals, which would give you the benefit of a change of scene from year to year: sweet peas, blue morning glory (*Ipomoea* 'Heavenly

Quick Tip

Where possible, straighten weather-beaten daffodils with leaves brought forward from behind the plant and tied in front with a reef-knot. *Mrs E J Barton*

Blue') or black-eyed Susan (*Thunbergia alata*), for example. The last two need spring sowing and warmth under glass until planting out in late May. Using annuals will also make it easier to access the forsythia for pruning after its spring flowering.

Looking Good in March ...

Camellias

Conveying the glamour of the Orient when in full bloom, camellias are robust, rewarding shrubs for gardens on neutral to acid soil. Many parts of the country are ideal for growing camellias; but if you live in a limestone or chalk area they are best grown in large tubs of ericaceous compost.

The *Camellia* x *williamsii* hybrids are rewarding, hardy garden plants with glossy foliage. 'Donation' is perhaps the most popular, not surprisingly, for it has sumptuous, Brighton-rock pink, rose-like blooms; 'Bridal Gown' has exquisite, pearly white flowers; 'Freedom Bell' forms a small, dense bush of sultry, deep red.

Woodland anemones

The dainty flowers of wood anemones make for pastel carpets that light up shady ground at this time of year. White or pale-pink *Anemone nemorosa* occurs naturally in Britain in deciduous woodland. In gardens, plant it in a sunny or partially shaded spot, around the base of a shrub, or among primroses, narcissi, hostas or peonies. Desirable garden forms of wood anemone include 'Vestal' with double white flowers, 'Allenii' with rosy flowers, and 'Bracteata Plena', with semi-double white flowers surrounded by a lacy green frill.

Wood anemones like humus-rich soil and plenty of compost; they are widely available at garden centres.

❋ NATURAL PEST CONTROL

If, like me, you're among the growing band of people who dislike using chemical pesticides in the garden, it is well worth considering the alternative: biological or 'natural' pest control. The principle of natural pest control is to create the conditions that will enable nature to deal with pests and infestations in its own way; in other words to introduce into the environment the insect pest's natural predators so that they can do the job for you.

Whitefly in the greenhouse, for example (which are in any case now resistant to many of the chemical sprays that were developed to deal with them), can be treated by introducing creatures that prey on them: one (which is used for bad infestations) is a tiny black ladybird called *Delphastus*; the other is an otherwise harmless black wasp, just 1mm long, called *Encarsia formosa*. When these predators are released into a greenhouse of adequately warm temperature, they can mop up whitefly most effectively and safely. However, several applications may be needed, and bear in mind that you cannot introduce them if you have recently used chemical sprays, for they – like other insects – are susceptible to them.

The wasps are easy to introduce, as they arrive on small cards that you then attach to infested plants; but, if you want to be sure of receiving them in time, order in March (*see* stockists opposite).

There are also creatures to control aphids under glass (the 2mm-long *Aphidius* parasite), and then there are *Phytoseiulus* mites (which prey on red spider-mite).

In the effort to combat the dreaded vine-weevil, considerable progress has been made in recent years. This weevil produces voracious, soil-dwelling larvae that can demolish all manner of treasured plants in very little time. (They are especially fond of fuchsias, begonias, cyclamen, primulas, and heucheras.) To deal with them there is a microscopic parasitic nematode called *Heterorhabditis*. Watering in this nematode when the weevil grubs are active ensures their destruction. For the weevil larvae to be active, however, the soil needs to be warm, so it is best to apply the nematode to outdoor or unheated-greenhouse soil between late spring and early autumn. In a heated greenhouse, it may be necessary to apply the nematodes in winter, too, as the artificial warmth will keep the larvae active.

Parasitic nematodes of a different type are used to combat slugs. These ones are especially useful where leafy crops and salads are being grown because – unlike chemicals – there is no risk of traces of poisonous bait being taken up by the plants. They work best on the smaller types of slug, which live in the soil; large slug species that dwell above ground level need to be trapped by some other means, as do snails (*see* pages 37–8).

New developments are being made all the time in the search for safe ways of controlling pests. With the help of pheromone traps, barrier glues, fleece and mesh crop-covering fabrics (all available from Chase Organics, *see* below), and the insect parasites mentioned above, it is possible to grow very good-quality flowers, fruits and vegetables without resorting to the use of dangerous sprays.

Mail-order stockists of the various types of trap and parasite include Green Gardener (tel. 01603 715096 includes Helpline), Defenders (tel. 01233 813121), Chase Organics (tel. 01932 253666), English Woodlands Biocontrol (tel. 01798 867574), and Agralan (tel. 01285 860015).

April

This month and next, the garden centres and nurseries do brisk trade as the nation wakes up to another gardening season. Some of us have been at it for a while, of course, but if you're only now venturing into the great outdoors then the nurseries have made it easy for you. We're spoilt for choice at this time of year, with vast quantities of potted bulbs, shrubs and early-flowering perennials. Some people frown at such 'instant gardening', but it's here to stay and if it enables more people to enjoy the garden, it must be a good thing.

ORNAMENTAL GARDEN

New Plants

As well as buying the plants that will provide interest in the coming month, don't forget the winter-flowering trees and shrubs. Often their prices are reduced now that their flowering is over, and are worth buying if in good condition.

New evergreens
This is a good time to plant evergreens, both hedging kinds and stand-alone shrubs: plant into well-prepared soil to which compost and some general fertiliser has been added.

Hedges
New hedges grow more quickly when they are not subjected to stress through lack of water in dry periods. Consider running a finely perforated 'seep-hose' along the length of a new hedge for the first couple of years until its roots are well established. These hoses work well in conjunction with programmable watering timers, which attach to the garden tap, but are less useful in hard-water areas where limescale may fur up the holes quite rapidly.

Magnolia magic
Magnolias look so good at this time of year that many people go out and buy one now. But choose its position with care: allow it plenty of space as it will strongly resent being moved later. Prepare the soil well, with plenty of leaf-mould, cocoa-shells, or a proprietary soil-conditioner/tree-planting compost. Water regularly over the coming months as the roots get established.

Rhododendrons
Favourite rhododendrons can be propagated by 'layering'. Peg down low-growing branches with a stone or wire hook so that part of the stem is resting on the soil surface. It will develop roots over the coming months, and can be separated from the parent plant this time next year. The technique also works with other shrubs, including elaeagnus,

syringa, skimmia, and magnolia. Making a slight wound in the stem (by nicking the bark) where it is to lay on the ground, and adding a touch of hormone rooting powder to it, helps the process.

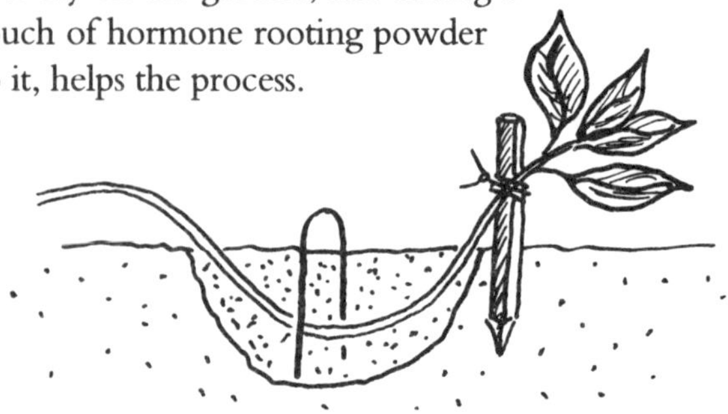

New gladioli

Gladioli are very easy to grow from corms planted now, 4-6 inches (10–15cm) deep in fertile, free-draining soil. As well as the buxom, Dame Edna Everage types, there are daintier species, such as *Gladiolus callianthus* (also known as *Acidanthera murieliae*), with white, pendent flowers, and *G. papilio* with small, nodding flowers flushed with mauve. All need a sunny position, but only the large-flowered hybrids need staking as they grow.

Hardy annuals

Sow hardy annuals to fill gaps. A light sprinkling of annual poppies or love-in-a-mist (*Nigella*) through the flowerbed can unify and enliven more sombre plantings, provided they have sunshine.

Scented stocks

To enjoy summer evening fragrance wafting in through open windows and doors you need to act now, and it could hardly be easier. Sow night-scented stocks (*Matthiola longipetala* or *M. bicornis*) by lightly scattering seeds over the soil wherever you want them to flower. The pale lilac-and-white blossoms are less showy than florists' stocks, but what they lack in flower stature is more than compensated by their ability to drench the air on midsummer evenings with deliciously sweet perfume.

Maintenance & Repair

Weather-watch
Continue checking weather forecasts for night temperatures and give vulnerable plants some covering protection with horticultural fleece, or old net curtains, when frost is expected.

Lawns
If any lawn repairs are needed, do them as soon as possible, with new turves or seed.

Privet
If you didn't get round to pruning the overgrown privet hedge last autumn, do it now. If very hard pruning is needed, do one side now and the other side next year, so as not to stress the plants too much. Then rake a slow-release general fertiliser into the soil surface beneath, and water in.

Faded flowers
Dead-head faded spring flowers and daffodils as soon as they fade so they don't waste their energy

❀ *Quick Tip* ❀

When potting on, first push the old, smaller pot into the new compost to make a hole the right size for the plant's root-ball. Then settle the plant into the perfectly fitting new hole. *B M Stratton*

producing seeds. Bulbs will benefit from the application of a liquid feed of general or phosphate-rich fertiliser to recharge them for next year.

Stray seedlings
Routinely check the ground for self-sown seedlings of garden plants: carefully dig them out and move them to a better position, if necessary, or pot them up for friends or for plant sales.

Plant supports
Ensure staking is in place for tall-growing herbaceous plants and herbs. Use canes and twine or proprietary wire plant supports.

KITCHEN GARDEN

Potatoes
Continue planting out potatoes, but cover the soil with a protective blanket of heavyweight horticultural fleece. Remember to leave some spare inches of fleece on either side, so there is room for the shoots to grow under its protection.

Asparagus
Asparagus is a long-term crop that can be productive for the next 20 years or so, and can be planted towards the end of this month. All-male varieties

such as 'Dariana' and 'Franklim' give the best crops, which can be harvested from the second year after planting. Soak one-year-old crowns for an hour before planting 6 inches (15cm) deep, 18 inches (45cm) apart, in a sunny bed well prepared with plenty of manure. Inside each planting hole, make a small mound of soil and spread the thick, spidery roots evenly over it. Cover the crowns with a little soil, and, when stems appear above the earth, add more soil. Continue adding soil as the stems grow until the ground is level again.

Brassicas
Plant out cabbages, cauliflower and Brussels sprouts sown last month. Fit brassica collars around plants to foil the cabbage-root flies, or grow them under Enviromesh fabric to keep away all types of pest.

INDOORS & UNDER GLASS

Young Plants

Plug-plants
Mail-ordered plug-plants are starting to arrive this month and need urgent attention. Pot them into fresh multi-purpose compost and keep them under glass for another month or so. They will grow steadily during warm, bright days but need shelter from drying winds and cool nights.

Tropical flowers
For late-season, tropical splendour – large, paddle-like leaves and showy flowers – pot up half-hardy *Canna* rhizomes in gritty potting compost and grow on in the greenhouse before bedding-out half-grown plants in June.

Citrus fruits
Pot on citrus-fruit trees into the next-sized pot, in free-draining John Innes No.3 compost with added sharp sand for extra drainage. The plant must be potted at the same depth as before: citrus trees have thin bark, which rots easily if transplanted trees are planted more deeply than they are used to. Wide selections of citrus fruits are available from Reads Nursery in Norfolk (tel. 01508 548395) and Global Orange Groves in Dorset (tel. 01202 826244).

Houseplants
Pot on houseplants into pots one or two sizes larger, with fresh proprietary compost. At the same time, check for pest damage and treat as necessary, and tidy up plants generally by cutting off any browned and damaged leaves at the base.

Shade

Put up movable shading in conservatories and greenhouses to protect plants from scorching on bright days. Provide daytime ventilation, especially whenever there is sunshine as temperatures warm up under glass very quickly.

❋ *Quick Tips* ❋

To clear moss from your lawn, place hens in a wire-run, and regularly move the run to different sections of lawn. The hens will scratch out the moss – and provide you with freshly laid eggs!
Mrs H Robinson

To stop any more mole-hills appearing, place half a raw onion face down on the hill opening.
Marjorie Cumming

Soil Pests

If plants are looking sickly, or dying for no obvious reason, check the rootball for plump, white vine-weevil grubs, which should be destroyed at once. Primulas, fuchsias, begonias, various succulents and evergreens are especially vulnerable, as are plants in pots (especially in the warmth of the greenhouse), but garden plants can be attacked, too. Once soil temperatures have reached 54°F (12°C) they can be treated with nematodes (*see* pages 44–5)

QUESTIONS & ANSWERS

We have recently made a fish-pond, now filled with tap-water. How soon can we start to put fish in it?

M Flynn, Carshalton

You haven't mentioned whether you have planted the pond yet, but plants must go in first (mid-April/May is an excellent time to introduce aquatics). Include some oxygenating plants; and some waterlilies for shade and hiding places. Fish supplied from an outdoor pool can be introduced in late April, those from an indoor pool in late May.

&

Some of my daffodils have grown, but not flowered this year. Why might this be?

John Wills, Glamorgan

There could be several reasons. They may be infested with eelworm, or they may have become too crowded. Or perhaps the bulbs were not planted deeply enough. Lift and divide the clumps and replant at the correct depth (three times the height of the bulb). Eelworm damage shows as brown rings through the bulbs, very noticeable when you cut a bulb in half horizontally. If this is the problem, dig up and destroy the bulbs, and plant new ones in a different place.

Looking Good in April ...

Grape hyacinths

Grape hyacinths (*Muscari* species) in blues and violets make wonderful companions to other flowers in mid-spring. They are small enough to fit into container displays and look particularly fine when grown with dwarf daffodils or the lemon-and-lime colours of *Euphorbia myrsinites*. As well as the popular *Muscari armeniacum*, look out for *M. latifolium*, with one broad leaf to each blue-violet flower spike; the dainty pale-blue *M. azureum*, and slender *M. botryoides* (which also has a white form, *M. b.* 'Alba'). These bulbs suit ordinary, well-drained soil, and need sunshine. Plant 2 inches (6cm) deep in early autumn.

Clematis

With its myriad starry flowers, the beautiful, early-flowering *Clematis montana* is a hearty, vigorous climber that will romp away over any suitable support of walling, trelliswork or trees. It comes in various shades from white to deep rose-pink, and it relishes deep, rich soil that's well fed with rotted manure or mushroom compost. When it becomes over-enthusiastic, prune it just after flowering has finished.

For a very small garden, *C. montana* is not the best choice because it will require quite a lot of attention in order to keep it within bounds. *C. alpina* and *C. macropetala* species are both delightful, spring-flowering, less rampant alternatives better suited to restricted conditions.

May

On the cusp of spring and summer, May can be cruelly deceptive. Bikini weather one day may be followed by boots and jacket temperatures the next. Horse-chestnuts in full leaf suggest that summer has arrived, but cherry blossom – along with the bluebells and lilacs – insist it's still spring. Then there are Spanish lavenders and flowering alliums that convey a sense of Mediterranean warmth. If you have a garden pond, this is the time to restock it with new plants. If you haven't – well, it's a good time to build one – but wait until the end of the month before bringing in new fish.

ORNAMENTAL GARDEN

Spring's Old Flowers

Any remaining spring bedding plants must be cleared away now. Fading tulip and daffodil foliage

looks awful, and in many instances the bulbs are best dug up and discarded; new ones, which are very cheap these days, can be planted in autumn. Alternatively, move existing ones to a spare piece of ground to finish ripening.

Primroses and polyanthus
Lift out and divide primroses and polyanthus that have finished flowering. Replant into soil enriched with some rotted organic compost.

Dead-heading
Dead-head spent blooms on early roses, irises and other early flowers wherever the seeds are not required for collection.

Summer Perennials

Nurseries and garden centres offer very good selections of container-grown hardy perennials at this time of year. Plant them out as soon as possible.

Roses
Check that roses are healthy. If you use chemical sprays, the recently reformulated Roseclear 2 works on both pests and typical rose diseases. The insecticide content destroys aphids, and is claimed to be harmless to beneficial insects such as bees, ladybirds and lacewings. However, ladybirds and their larvae need to eat, so spraying should be strictly confined to plants that really do need it.

Clematis
Clematis can be propagated now from cuttings. Take a section of vigorous stem and cut it about 2 inches (5cm) below a leaf-joint. Trim the top of

the cutting just above the single pair of leaves. Dip the base into hormone rooting powder, and pot up in proprietary seed and cuttings compost. Cover with clear polythene and set in a warm place in natural light, but away from direct sunlight. Rooting takes several weeks.

Support for climbers
Check that climbers and tall-growing herbaceous plants have adequate supports in place. Carefully tie in to their support any wayward shoots on summer- and autumn-flowering clematis.

Tie in new shoots springing out of rambler and climbing roses, wrapping them spirally around posts and wig-wams, or training horizontally along wires on fences and walls. The more horizontal you can get the stems, the more prolific their production of flowers will be.

Annuals

Thin out the seedlings from earlier sowings of hardy annuals. If you missed the boat earlier, don't worry – there is still time to sow some annual flowers to brighten up the summer. If you're out all day, concentrate on those that are at their best in the evening: fragrant night-scented stocks, white-flowered *Cosmos* 'Purity', and annual evening primroses (*Oenothera odorata*) whose brilliant-lemon flowers open at dusk to enable moths to pollinate

❋ ***Quick Tip*** ❋

When building an arch or garden path, try to make it wide enough for two people to walk comfortably side-by-side. *L Furniss*

them. Simply scatter the seeds (available from Chilterns, tel. 01229 581137) thinly in weed-free ground, wherever you want them to flower.

Sweet-peas
Sweet-peas can also still be sown directly where they are to flower. They make a rapid seasonal covering for a less-than-pretty fence, and coil their tendrils around any given support with ease. (Pick flowers regularly to keep the plants in bloom – they stop flowering if allowed to go to seed.)

Hedges & Topiary

Give box hedging and topiaries their first trim in early May (but wait until the end of the month in cold regions). Use sharp shears (or powered hedge-trimmers on long runs of hedging). If necessary, another cut can be given in late summer to maintain the plants' crisp outline for the winter. (*See also* page 110.)

Quick Tip

A kettle of boiling water works wonders on weeds in paths and patio cracks. *Dorothy Smith*

Water & Containers

Ensure plants are receiving adequate water; pay special attention to containers. May can sometimes be quite drizzly, without there actually being enough water to supply a plant's needs.

Weeds

Weed growth is prolific now, so hoe out annual weeds regularly. Take advantage of any periods following rain when the soft ground makes it easier to dig out perennial and tap-rooted weeds.

Lawn weeds

I am fairly tolerant of weeds such as daisies and tiny blue speedwell because I like them. But if you don't, and you yearn for a weed-free sward, now is the best time to apply a proprietary weed-and-feed treatment (following the maker's instructions). The odd weed can be tackled by damaging it and then pouring salt into the rosette, but it's important not to spill salt on the grass at the same time.

Pests & Diseases

Slugs, snails and aphids

Soft, new growth is very vulnerable to attack by slugs, snails and aphids. Gently rub aphids off plants with finger and thumb; inspect slug and snail roosting places, and empty them out each morning.

Caterpillars

Some plants, such as mulleins (*Verbascum*), are very susceptible to caterpillar damage from now on. Check the leaves for mullein-moth caterpillars, and remove them before they rapidly demolish your plants.

Lily beetles
Bright-scarlet lily beetles (just ¼ inch/7mm long), are destructive pests and well worth making the effort to hunt them down. You'll find them now, lurking among the leaves and flowerheads of lilies and fritillaries. Their larvae are less easy to spot as they cover themselves with their own black faeces. Both the adults and the larvae are capable of ruining a plant by munching through leaves, flowers and seedpods. Pick them off and crush them.

Ponds

Plant out pond plants in aquatic compost that is low in nutrients (a high nutrient content encourages the development of algae). Before submerging plants, cover the soil with grit to avoid soil disturbance by fish. Overgrown waterlilies and other aquatics should be lifted and divided now.

KITCHEN GARDEN

Sowing & Planting

Sow French and runner beans, beetroot, carrots, parsnips and salad crops outdoors. Fortnightly successional sowings of short rows will provide crops over a longer period and avoid those sudden gluts when everything crops together. Continue sowing salads, peas, summer cabbage and cauliflower, beetroots and turnips. Also sow sweetcorn, marrows and courgettes.

Harden off tomatoes, peppers, aubergines, courgettes and squashes, providing protection from cold night temperatures. In mild areas they can be planted outdoors from mid-May, into fertile, well-prepared ground.

Beans
Sow heavy cropping stringless runner beans such as white-flowered 'Mergoles' or early-podding 'Polestar'. Growing sweet-peas among them makes bean rows more decorative. The dwarf runner bean 'Pickwick' grows as a short bush, useful for exposed gardens or for growing under protection.

French beans sown last month in warmth can be planted out now 6 inches (15cm) apart; cover them with fleece overnight if the weather turns cold.

Sweetcorn
Plant out young sweetcorn from mid-May (but delay a couple of weeks in cold areas). Plant in blocks of a dozen or more, to get even pollination, spacing plants about 15 inches (38cm) apart in each direction. You can also sow corn seeds directly into fertile, well-manured ground, in an open, sunny, sheltered site. Sow two or three to each planting space, thin out the weakest, and water regularly.

Herbs from seed
Sow basil, coriander, dill and culinary fennel directly into the garden in sunny, free-draining soil.

❀ *Quick Tips* ❀

To clear a pond of blanket weed, twirl a sturdy rough twig in the water and wind out the weed that sticks to it. *Mrs M Pickles*

To assist birds or frogs that fall into outdoor water-butts or tanks, float a piece of wood on the surface. *Mrs B A Combe*

To deter cats visiting nestboxes, paint a small surrounding area regularly with honey. *M Tonkin*

Bear in mind that the last three should be grown apart from each other to reduce the risk of cross-pollination between them, which results in poor quality seeds.

Make fortnightly sowings of rocket into rich soil in an open or semi-shaded site.

Herbs ready-grown

There are tray-loads of tempting herbs on sale at garden shops now, so even if you don't want to sow your own, there is no excuse for not having home-grown leaves to use in the kitchen. If you grow them in pots, choose a sunny terrace or windowsill and plant into John Innes No.3 compost, which is free-draining and easy for roots to settle into. No herb garden should be without rosemary, thyme, mint and lavender, and basil can go outdoors from the end of May.

Fruit

Strawberries

Tuck clean straw or strawberry mats around strawberry plants to protect the fruits from mud-splashes and to help conserve moisture in the soil.

Wall Fruit

Check that fruit trees trained against walls are receiving adequate water, as the soil beside walls is likely to be much drier than elsewhere.

❃ *Quick Tip* ❃

To prevent bamboo canes from splitting, put a spent gun-cartridge over the end of the cane before hammering it into the ground. *Mrs J Price*

Pests

Blackfly

Blackfly clustering around the tips of broad beans are best removed by pinching off the affected shoot tips and squashing them under foot.

Moths

Codling moths attack apple and pear trees from the start of May. Pheromone traps (*see* pages 44–5) attract the roving male moths, bringing them to a sticky end before they can find the females and fertilise eggs. This means fewer maggots to attack the fruit. One kit protects one to four trees. Replace the sticky sheet and pheromone after six weeks.

Plum-fruit moths attack damsons and gages, as well as plums, and separate pheromone traps are available for these. One trap protects one to three trees. Check all pheromone traps at the end of the month to monitor the quantity of male moths being caught.

INDOORS & UNDER GLASS

Summer Flowers

Morning glory (*Ipomoea* 'Heavenly Blue'), whose brilliant-azure trumpets are so evocative of Mediterranean holidays, must be sown every year (in about mid-May): soak seeds overnight, then sow three per 4-inch (10cm) pot, half an inch (1.5 cm) deep. Keep them at around 68°F/20°C (the seedlings go weak and pale if they are subjected to any chill). Plant out in mid-June.

Pot on summer flowers, including petunias, verbenas, salvias, calendulas, under glass. Those that are not being grown on for outdoor pots and baskets can be grown to maturity in attractive pots for temporary indoor decoration later on.

Tomatoes

Feed growing tomatoes regularly with high-potash fertiliser to encourage good flowering and fruiting.

Shade

Greenhouse plants need protection from too much sunshine in fine weather. An exterior coating of Coolglass shade paint (sold in garden centres) considerably reduces temperatures, and all vents should be kept open during bright days. Even so, a fan may also be necessary.

Whitefly Cure

For an organic deterrent to whitefly, plant aromatic annual tagetes (widely available now, in bedding-plant packs) among tomatoes. Use two tagetes for each tomato plant.

Houseplants

On a mild day, give houseplants a spring clean by standing them in the shower and gently spraying the foliage with tepid water. Then put them outdoors for a few hours in the middle of the day, but not where they can be scorched by hot sunshine. Most shiny-leaved houseplants can be treated

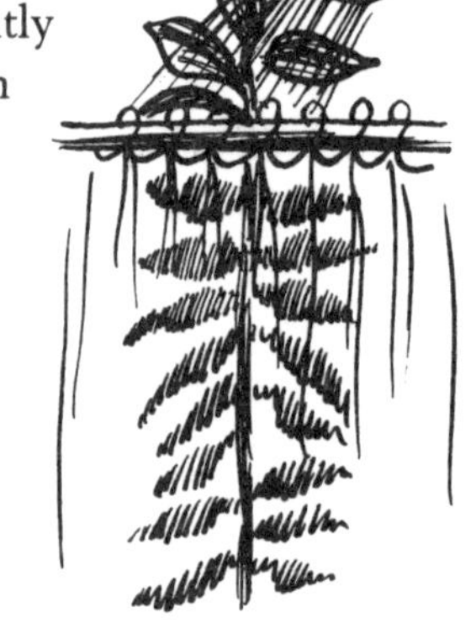

this way, but not those with hairy leaves, such as African violets, which would rot.

QUESTIONS & ANSWERS

I'd like to turn part of our large garden into a semi-wild area, with long grass and wildflowers. Where can I get the right sort of grass-seed and plants?

K Simms, Bolton

Successful establishment of wildflower and grass mixtures depends on your garden's soil type and aspect. For example, a mixture suitable for sunny, dry soils will be different from one intended for damp soils in shady positions.

Suffolk Herbs (tel. 01376 572456) has a large selection of grass- and wildflower-seed mixes suitable for different needs, all chosen specifically to encourage butterflies, bees, birds, and other wildlife. British Wild Flower Plants at Great Yarmouth (tel. 01493 730244), sells as pot-grown or plug-plant wildflowers grown from seed.

What can I plant in a narrow bed, beside the fence, which gets sunlight for only a very brief period in the morning? I have tried a few flowers, but have not been able to achieve any sort of display to be proud of.

Cynthia Green, Norwich

Plants that relish shade for most of the day include ferns, hostas, and winter-to-spring-flowering hellebores. Annual tobacco plants (*Nicotiana* varieties), in pretty colours of lime-green, crimson, pink and white, will bloom all summer; *Nicotiana alata grandiflora*, though unremarkable by day, unfurls its fluted white trumpets at dusk to release a heady perfume. Or try epimediums, whose polished leaves reflect light as well as excluding weeds, or lungworts (*Pulmonaria*), with their white-spotted leaves and early-spring flowers. Ensure the soil is fertile and, if necessary, work in plenty of well-rotted manure to enrich it.

I understand that cardoons were popular vegetables in Victorian times. I'd love to grow some but I'm not sure where to get them from, or how to go about it.

B McCann, Southampton

Cardoons (*Cynara cardunculus*) are long-lived perennials closely related to the globe artichoke, and you can buy seeds from Suffolk Herbs (tel. 01376 572456). Some people grow them in the herbaceous border for their huge rosettes of silvery (rather prickly) leaves and large, thistly flowers. Sow the seeds in mid-spring in well-manured, free-draining soil in a sunny position. Water regularly through the season, as they grow quickly.

If you want to eat them, you'll need to 'blanch' them before harvesting them: on a dry day in early autumn, draw together the stems and leaves while the plant's still in the ground, and tie them. Wrap them in newspaper, sacking or straw to exclude

Quick Tip

To water delicate, newly sown seeds without disturbing them, squeeze water from a soaked cotton-wool ball. *R Phellas*

light, tie with raffia, and leave for three to five weeks. You can then eat the pale stalks and midribs of the inner leaves – cook as you would celery.

Looking Good in May ...

Californian lilacs

Draped in showers of Delft-blue blooms, the Californian lilacs (*Ceanothus* species) make a stunning show this month. They're not really lilacs at all, but they do come from California and its neighbouring states. Their origins are a clue to their preference for a hot spot; they can't tolerate extreme cold. A position near the shelter of a south- or west-facing wall suits them, and they like fertile, freely draining soil. The many excellent varieties of evergreen ceanothus in flower this month include 'Delight', 'Concha' and the evocatively named 'Italian Skies', all with glorious deep-blue flowers on undemanding, substantial shrubs. They don't like heavy pruning, however, so be sure to give them plenty of room, and only lightly prune (if really necessary) just after flowering has finished.

Candelabra primulas

If you have an area of moisture-retentive soil in light shade or sun, you could enjoy the splendour of candelabra primulas, which come from the Far East. They are so named because of the way the flowers are arranged in whorls up the stems, giving a brilliant, tiered effect. *Primula bulleyana* has pale-orange flowers in early May, while *P. prolifera* is a lemon-yellow. For striking drifts of magenta, choose *P. japonica*, best in shade; its white form, 'Postford White', makes a pleasing contrast among the deeper pinks.

June

In June we have the longest days of the year (in terms of sunlight, anyway) and the month when we can perhaps derive the most pleasure – and the most produce – from the garden. If you're out at work all day, make sure you have plenty of white and pale-blue flowers around because these are the ones that will glow ethereally as the light fades. Evening primrose, with its acid-yellow petals opening at dusk and yielding their fragrance, are worth having, too.

ORNAMENTAL GARDEN

Continue a regular programme of watering, weeding, and checking plants for pests and disease.

New Plants

Late annuals
There's still time to sow a few quick-maturing, hardy annuals – such as *Godetia*, *Clarkia*, stocks and calendulas – to fill late-season gaps.

Penstemons
Amongst the worthwhile perennials that will be on sale this month are penstemons, including the pale, mauve-blue 'Stapleford Gem', 'Hidcote Pink' and the burgundy-wine-coloured 'Blackbird'. They are ideal for enlivening bare bits of ground and, given a sunny, well-drained spot, many flower prolifically through the summer.

Daphnes
Daphnes can be quite difficult to propagate, but cuttings taken now often prove successful. Use 3–4 inch (8–10cm) long, non-flowering shoots, potted up into freely draining seed-and-cuttings compost. Some patience is called for, as rooting may take three months or more.

Pond plants
Finish planting new aquatics into garden ponds.

Pruning & Dead-heading

Tidy up alyssum, aubrieta, and any other rapidly spreading, prostrate spring-flowering plants by trimming them with shears after flowering.

Dead-head faded early summer flowers, such as irises and peonies, leaving the species whose seeds will be wanted. Follow up with a dressing of general fertiliser spread over the soil. Pinch out growing tips of later summer bedding, such as *Impatiens* (busy Lizzies), fuchsias, petunias and verbenas, to encourage bushier growth.

Trees, shrubs and hedges
Prune philadelphus, spiraea, deutzia and *Ribes* bushes as soon as flowering has finished. Also prune overgrown spring-flowering viburnums if necessary. The softwood tips can be used as cuttings.

Trim fast-growing hedges such as *Lonicera nitida*, cypress species, and privet. If you didn't trim box hedging last month, now is a good time to do it.

Mulching, Watering & Feeding

It's not too late to lay mulches around drought-hating plants, such as dahlias, if you didn't do it earlier. Composted-bark and cocoa-shell mulches help conserve soil moisture and improve soil texture. Lay mulch quite thickly (2–3 inches/5–8cm deep) over recently watered soil.

Ensure that all plants are adequately watered, keeping a special eye on all trees and shrubs planted in the last year, and plants and climbers close to walls (as walls tend to leach water from the soil). It is impossible to know in June whether the rest of the summer will be dry, but with the holiday period looming, consider buying an automatic irrigation system (widely available in garden and DIY shops), with a controlled time-switch. When properly used they are very economical with water, and some kits are designed to water plants grouped together in containers.

Acid-lovers
Ericaceous shrubs (such as rhododendrons, azaleas and pieris) growing in containers or raised beds will

need feeding. Water in a solution of the seaweed-based Maxicrop Plus Sequestered Iron, or Miracid.

Bedding plants
When planting out summer bedding and young perennials, water them well first to ensure that their rootballs are not dry when they go into the soil. Then, to give them a good start, water them in with a weak liquid feed rather than plain water.

Sweet-peas
Cut sweet-pea flowers regularly to promote continued flowering, and water with a proprietary liquid feed every ten days or so. Ensure each plant is receiving adequate water and, if the weather is very dry, mulch the soil surface after watering.

Dahlias
Apply a weekly liquid feed, and prevent earwigs reaching the flowers by painting the stem with a band of petroleum jelly or insect barrier glue.

Pests & Diseases

Pollen-beetles
Before bringing cut flowers indoors, check for pollen-beetles, the tiny black insects that infest flowerheads. To get rid of them, place affected flowers in a dark corner of the shed or garage for a couple of hours, and the beetles will fly out to the light of the window or open door.

❋ *Quick Tip* ❋

To remove greenfly from roses brought into the house, blow with a cool hairdrier. *P Walken*

Vine-weevils
Now is a good time to water in a nematode biological control (*see* pages 44–5) around potential vine-weevil banquets, which include succulents, primulas, lilies, heucheras, yews, viburnums, and many evergreen shrubs).

Clematis wilt
If your clematis is struck by wilt, cut the stems to the ground and burn them. Watering in fungicide may help to encourage new shoots. To avoid wilt, consider growing late-flowering *C. viticella* varieties, as these are generally not susceptible.

KITCHEN GARDEN

Thin out vegetable and flower seedlings to their appropriate final spacings. And continue planting out tomatoes, sweetcorn, courgettes, marrows, runner beans, celery, and ridge cucumbers.

Fruits

Make sure that soft fruit, and apple and pear trees, are receiving regular water, and harvest the fruit the moment it is ripe. Apple trees naturally shed a load of half-developed fruit at this time. Further thinning may not be required unless large fruits (such as 'Bramley' cookers) are required.

Herbs

Make fresh sowings of basil and coriander in a sunny, well-drained part of the garden. Pinch out the flowering tips regularly to maintain bushy, leafy growth. Clumps of mint, growing so strongly now, can be divided and replanted, but it is best grown in well-watered pots, or open-bottomed buckets plunged into the ground, as it is very invasive.

Asparagus

After the final harvest, feed your asparagus plants with a general organic fertiliser to restore vigour in

the crowns underground. Leave the ferns to grow up for the rest of the season.

INDOORS & UNDER GLASS

Continue potting on greenhouse and houseplants and planting up outdoor containers. Potted shrubs may need to be transferred to larger containers or at least given a top-dressing of fresh compost and some slow-release feed.

Early this month, plant peppers and aubergines in larger pots or growing-bags. Ensure they get the sunniest part of the greenhouse and plenty of ventilation; plug in a fan on bright days, if necessary.

❋ ***Quick Tip*** ❋

Train bindweed up a cane to keep it away from other plants before applying weedkiller to it. Mrs L Marchant

Feeding & Watering

Continue regular watering in the greenhouse and conservatory. Plants need daily attention during sunny, dry spells. Check that shade has been provided, for any plants that need it.

Tomatoes

To encourage fruit setting of tomatoes, tap the flowers lightly to release pollen. Spraying the plants lightly with a mist of water each day to increase the humidity around the blooms will assist pollination.

Cacti

In warm spells, move housebound cacti outdoors to a bright but sheltered position so they can enjoy some fresh air and extra sunlight. Increase watering to once or twice weekly (even more frequently in very hot, dry weather), especially if the pots are very small. Although cacti are desert plants, and therefore have the reputation of tolerating drought, the confines of a pot mean that their water needs are considerable during growth. To encourage the development of flowers feed fortnightly with weak liquid high-potash fertiliser (such as a tomato feed).

Cuttings

Take softwood cuttings of lithodora, helianthemums, perennial wallflowers (such as *Erysimum* 'Bowles Mauve'), and *Convolvulus cneorum.* Use a sharp knife to make a clean cut at the base of one of this year's healthy, non-flowering shoots. Cut off lower leaves cleanly, pot up, and water in with fungicide solution and cover pot with polythene.

Pests

Red spider-mites can be difficult to see, but their numbers quickly build up under glass in warm weather. Some control can be achieved by regularly hosing down paths and staging during hot, dry spells to increase the humidity. Increase air circulation by opening vents and doors. The predatory mite *Phytoseiulus persimilis* is an effective biological control (*see* pages 44–5) provided pesticides have not already been used.

QUESTIONS & ANSWERS

I would love to dry some of the lavender in my garden. What's the best way of doing it?

C Sharp, Beckenham

Pick the flowers just before they are fully open, early on a fine day, when the dew has dried off. Tie them in small bunches and hang them upside-

❃ *Quick Tip* ❃

Sow poppy seed among raspberry canes. In summer, the birds will confuse the red flowers for berries and leave far more fruit. *Mrs L Bradley*

down in an airy place, away from direct sunlight. When the flowers are crisp to the touch, they are ready. Either keep them on their stems to display, or strip them off the stalks to use in pot-pourri.

ℰ𝒪

Can I prune my deciduous azaleas and, if so, when would be the best time to do it?

Ed Jones, Lyndhurst

Deciduous azaleas do not usually need pruning unless they become too large for their home, in which case prune as soon as the flowers are over (usually June). Shorten stems by up to half their length, cutting just above a leaf-bud. Very old stems may be cut out completely at the base – a good thing to do occasionally to invigorate the plant.

ℰ𝒪

A few months ago I was given a beautifully fragrant Stephanotis *houseplant. Now its leaves are turning yellow and many have dropped off. Can I save it?*

M Appleby, Weymouth

It sounds as if dryness at the roots (and almost certainly in the atmosphere, too), is the cause of your problems. The remedy is to pot on into a slightly larger pot of suitable houseplant compost, and ensure the soil is never allowed to dry out completely. Stand the pot on a tray of wet pebbles, so that moisture can evaporate into the air around the plant. Keep the plant in a room with an even temperature, away from draughts and sunny windows.

Check for signs of spider-mite damage (microscopic pests that spin fine 'webs' around stems and under leaves). Spray affected plants with a proprietary house-plant spray.

Looking Good in June ...

Perennial peonies

Through the month of June the flowers of the peony are a visual tonic: from tight little golf-ball buds burst satiny petals in brilliant shades ranging from white through pale and rich rose-pink, to deep red and crimson. The peony ranks among the oldest of cultivated flowers (their roots have been used in traditional Chinese medicine for at least 1,500 years). Over the centuries many cultivars have been bred, but the peony became especially fashionable in Europe at the close of the 19th century when there was renewed interest in all things oriental.

Peonies like well-drained soil in full sun (although they can tolerate a little shade), and are easy to grow once they have settled in. They are very long-lived, seldom fall prey to the more common garden pests and, if left undisturbed, will perform well for scores of years. Specialist suppliers include Kelways Ltd (tel. 01458 250521) and Claire Austin Hardy Plants (tel. 01902 376333).

Day-lilies

With large blooms bursting forth from clumps of slender, arching foliage, day-lilies (*Hemerocallis* varieties) are among the most rewarding of midsummer perennials. Each flower lasts just a day, hence the popular name, but they produce many on each stem and over a long season. What they lack in scent, they make up for with their beautiful blooms. Day-lilies come in a huge range of colours, particularly yellows, reds and warm, russet tones, and grow well in most soils and conditions, except deep shade. Dig out and divide the clumps every few years in early spring.

❃ POTTED PERFECTION

Potted plants make the pleasures and satisfaction of gardening accessible to everyone: even if you don't have a garden there will be a windowsill, a stretch of wall, a balcony, or even a flight of steps where you can put a pot – or even several.

The secret's in the soil

The range of excellent potting composts available means that provided you water and feed your plants, success is virtually assured. Garden centres stock a bewildering array: 'multi-purpose', ericaceous, peat-free, soil-based, and certified organic types, plus specialist mixes for seeds and cuttings, trees and shrubs, houseplants, cacti, and hanging baskets. And there is now 'Plant Protection' compost, which contains insecticide to kill pests such as aphids and vine-weevils. So where do you start?

Potting composts can be divided first of all into two types: loamless and loam-based. Loamless (soil-less) types are made with non-soil materials (most frequently peat). However, as people have discovered that irreplaceable peat-bogs are being destroyed in the process of making loamless compost, peat-free alternatives made from coir-fibre (a by-product of the coconut industry), or from shredded bark or recycled waste materials, are now popular, and generally of better quality than they used to be. Loam-based types, usually sold under the John Innes name, are made of sterilised soil and smaller amounts of peat and grit, plus fertilisers. John Innes No.1 and Seed composts are low in nutrients; No.2 has double the fertiliser of No.1, and No.3 is an even richer mixture for gross feeders such as potted vegetables and mature plants and shrubs.

Loam-based compost is much heavier than its soil-less counterpart – an advantage where stability is important (for patio pots and those containing large shrubs or topiarised trees, for example). It is very free-draining, making it good for alpines, herbs, and succulents, and so on, but one of its greatest advantages is that it re-wets easily, which is very helpful if you are apt to miss out on watering now and again.

Being lighter, soil-less composts are usually best for hanging baskets, wall pots, and for those who find lifting heavy pots difficult. Peat-based kinds are notoriously difficult to re-wet when they have dried out, and coir-based ones can look very dry on the surface when there is still plenty of moisture lower down in the pot (so it is important not to overwater coir).

Whichever type you choose, go for a good-quality brand. And it is worth mixing in some water-retaining gel crystals (sold in garden centres), which help roots to tap into a source of moisture if they need it.

Pots of style

There are many different types of pot: plastic, terracotta, lead, faux-lead, glazed clay, gleaming metal, stone, wirework, and wood. So think about the general theme of your garden before making a choice. To enhance the romantic cottage garden, for example, rustic wood and plain terracotta pots suit; for the streamlined, modernist approach, shiny metal planters are appropriate. Some glazed pots are distinctly oriental in style, while others, such as the beautiful Anduze vases, are Mediterranean in character.

Beware of pots that curve inwards at the top: they're fine for regularly changed displays, such as bedding plants, but not for long-term plantings of perennials and shrubs because at repotting time you won't be able to remove the rootball without breaking the pot. Square pots hold more compost than round ones of equivalent width as there is all that corner space to fill; these are the better choice for plants with extensive, hungry roots. When buying window-boxes, choose the largest possible size that will fit on the sill so that you can create a really worthwhile display. Remember, too, that to avoid accidents any pots raised off the ground must be properly secured.

Feeding & watering

The fertiliser in potting compost is usually used up within six weeks, so add slow-release fertiliser granules to the compost at potting time, or give a liquid feed every week or two through the growing season.

Container plants are especially vulnerable to drought: the pot imposes a limit on the depth to which the roots can grow in search of moisture, and the heat of the sun on the pot's side speeds the drying process. If there is no one to water the garden and pick fruit while you are on holiday, group pots together in a shady position, open to the rain, and give them a good soak before you leave. Consider buying a mini watering system that can be set to work at regular intervals.

Repotting

Some plants need potting on every year or two (in spring) into slightly larger pots. Always replant into fresh compost; if the rootball is congested, carefully loosen the fibrous outer roots with a hand-fork, and prune some of the thicker roots if necessary. Note that some plants (e.g. figs and agapanthus), perform best when their roots are constricted.

July

Some people cannot be drawn from their gardens at this time of year, and who can blame them? There's certainly plenty to do if you've a mind to and, if you haven't, plenty to look at from the comfort of a garden seat or hammock. It is also a good month to go garden visiting. So much can be learned from strolling through the gems of gardens that open to the public just one or two afternoons a year for charity.

ORNAMENTAL GARDEN

Pruning, Trimming, Dead-heading

Cut off any rotting flowerbuds spoiled by rain, and continue dead-heading spent blooms. Ensure dahlia stems have cane supports. If you prefer

large, single blooms on dahlias, remove competing flowerbuds by snapping off side ones and retaining the central, largest bud.

Wisteria
It's time to give wisteria a summer pruning. Cut back the long, green whippy shoots, leaving four or five leaf-joints remaining on each stem.

Hedges and topiaries
Continue trimming hedges and topiaries. Shaped bay trees are best trimmed with secateurs rather than with hedging shears, as the large leaves look unsightly when cut in two.

Roses
Rose-suckers emanate from the rootstock and usually look quite different from the branches of the main plant. Pull off any suckers at the base, even this means having to delve into the soil to find the sucker's growth point on the root.

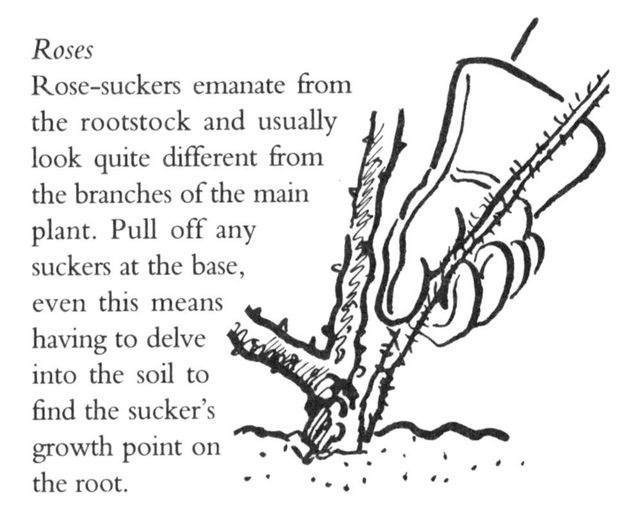

New Plants

Autumn bulbs
Towards the end of the month, plant colchicums and autumn crocuses into well-prepared soil and water in. A couple of weeks later, water with a weak solution of potash-rich fertiliser.

Cuttings
Take cuttings of rock-garden plants, shrubby herbs and half-hardy perennials.

Irises
Lift and divide large clumps of bearded iris after flowering. Tease clumps apart, using a sharp knife to cut through thick sections of root. Divide them into smaller pieces, leaving one or two fans of leaves to each root. Trim these leaves to about half their original height, and then replant the rhizome just below soil level, preferably facing south so the sun can bake it.

Watering & Feeding

Water continues to be the watch word: check that all new plantings, including any trees and shrubs planted within the last 12 months, are receiving adequate water. Maintain a regular watering programme for plants in containers and under glass.

Late summer's flowers
To encourage good flowering, feed agapanthus and dahlias with general-purpose fertiliser, followed by a weak solution of tomato fertiliser a week later.

Lavenders
Boost lavender plants with a liquid feed of organic general fertiliser such as Maxicrop. If you intend to dry some lavender, wait until the flowers are show-

ing colour but not yet fully opened; on a dry day, cut off whole flower stems, then tie the stalks together and hang upside-down in a cool place.

Pests & Diseases

Lilies
Continue to check lilies for scarlet lily-beetles, which should be picked off and destroyed.

Bay trees
Bay suckers (the sap-feeding insects that cause yellowed, distorted and curled leaves at the shoot tips) are prevalent at this time of year. Routine pruning will remove many of them. Insecticides can be effective but will also poison bees and other beneficial insects; they are in any case undesirable if the leaves are to be used for cooking (although manufacturers usually give instructions on recommended intervals between spraying and harvesting).

Bees
Leaf-cutting bees are active early in the month, taking large, semi-circular 'bites' out of leaves, usually from one favoured plant (soft-leaved shrubs such as *Hypericum*, roses, amelanchier, wisteria and others are susceptible). These bees are useful pollinators, so spraying with insecticide is not desirable, but badly affected plants will benefit from a light feed.

Mildew damage
Downy mildew thrives in summers plagued by frequent rain. Remove infected leaves and increase air circulation around plants by removing weeds and ensuring that plants are not too close to each other. If necessary, spray with a suitable fungicide.

KITCHEN GARDEN

New Plants

Summer sowings
Sow spring cabbages now for harvesting from February onwards. Sow quick-maturing (early) peas to ensure rapid crop development in the late season. Continue sowing salads.

Young leeks
Transplant pencil-thin leek seedlings into their final positions in vertical holes 6 inches (15cm) apart and around 8 inches (20cm) deep. Water in.

Strawberries
To get new strawberry plants from old, peg down runners that are producing little plantlets, using a stone or bent piece of wire to hold them in place. Once rooted, they can be severed from the parent and transplanted. Remove any unwanted runners to maintain vigour in the older plants.

Summer Harvest

Harvest herbs such as rosemary, lavender, oregano, and hang them in bunches, upside-down, in a cool, airy room. When they are fully dried, store them in jars for winter use.

Continue harvesting broad beans, globe artichokes, shallots, early potatoes, dwarf French beans, early runner beans, and carrots.

Drying shallots

Lift and dry shallots that were planted early in the year. Drying outdoors is practical only if there is no likelihood of rain; otherwise lay them out on the greenhouse bench where the air can circulate freely. After two to four weeks, they can be stored in the shed or garage between sheets of newspaper.

Mulching & Pruning

Fruit

Summer-prune wall-trained apples: cut the thin, whippy branches of this year's growth back to four or five buds to encourage fruiting spurs. This will also remove most aphids, which feed on the tender shoot tips. Start pruning cherries and plums.

Tomatoes

Nip out side-shoots from cordon-trained tomato plants regularly.

Runner beans

Provide runner beans with a thick mulch of well-rotted manure. To help their flowers to set and crop, mist them with tepid water every evening.

Herbs
Cut back leggy stems of mint, and pinch out tips of basil, lemon balm and oregano to encourage bushy new growth. Regularly remove flower-stalks of coriander, unless you are growing them for seeds.

Caterpillar Damage

Check plants – especially cabbages and peas – for signs of caterpillars, and destroy any that you find. Pea-moth catepillars are most active during the main growing season, so they are best avoided by growing early- or late-season varieties.

INDOORS & UNDER GLASS

Shade & Air

Provide shade and ventilation for greenhouse tomatoes and other crops as needed.

Revitalise housebound *Cymbidium* orchids by setting them outdoors in a partially shaded position for the next few weeks, where they can enjoy fresh air and rainwater. (As for any containerised plants, though, water them regularly if the weather is dry.)

New Plants

Cuttings
Take cuttings of lavender, rosemary and sage. Pot up, and place them in a shaded part of the greenhouse, or a shady cold-frame.

❋ ***Quick Tip*** ❋

Sprinkle cloves, or oil of cloves, around areas plagued by red ants. *C Chaplin*

Take cuttings of box and hydrangea, the latter from non-flowering shoots.

Seeds
Sow seeds of next year's flowers: biennials such as Iceland poppies, Brompton stocks, wallflowers, sweet-williams, and pansies.

Potting on
Pot on begonias, fuchsias and other greenhouse or conservatory plants that were started off in spring.

QUESTIONS & ANSWERS

The old-fashioned English roses I bought two years ago look nice and healthy but do not flower very well.

J Birch, Sudbury

They may need more sunshine (but don't move them until around November when they are settling into winter dormancy). Roses like well-fed, well-manured, freely draining soil, but not too much nitrogen (which encourages leaf growth at the expense of flowers). A proprietary rose and shrub fertiliser should help.

The hedgehogs in our garden do useful work keeping the slugs down, but one of them very narrowly missed being executed by the strimmer recently. Is there any way we can protect our prickly friends while tending the garden?

Fred Turner, Newbury

Strimmers are perhaps the most common cause of injury to hedgehogs, so do check long grass and undergrowth very carefully before strimming. The warmth of compost attracts nesting hedgehogs, so take care when turning the compost heap; and ensure that your pond has a sloping side or plank of wood that will provide a means of escape for any thirsty hedgehogs that fall in. Hedgehogs are marvellous garden allies: they are worth looking after.

Gardening experts say that woodlice do no harm, but my garden is full of them, and I have certainly seen them eating perfectly healthy plants.

M J Brown, Eastbourne

There are several chemical bait powders that will kill woodlice, but these are usually toxic to other, more beneficial garden wildlife, too. Instead, remove most of the debris that is providing food and shelter for them – unused pots, stray rocks, wood-piles, plus rotten plant material or discarded prunings. Leave one or two places as traps, which you must deal with regularly until they are under control. Prevent them reaching plants on greenhouse benches by putting a band of grease or insect glue-trap around the bench legs.

❋ Quick Tips ❋

Garden mint relieves nettle-stings faster than a dock-leaf does. *Mrs J Worthington*

A spray of hair lacquer will prevent pollen or leaves falling from cut flowers. *Wendy Brooks*

For longer-lasting cut flowers, water plants the the night before cutting, and cut them in the early morning or late evening. *Dr M Grange*

Looking Good in July ...

Sea-hollies

Spiky and spectacular, the sea-hollies (eryngiums), make wonderful border plants as well as cut and dried flowers. The hardy perennial *Eryngium x oliverianum* is one of the loveliest, with a metallic-blue sheen to its stems and branched heads of flowers. *E. bourgatii* has a steely-blue sheen shot through with silver, and *E. planum* has many small flowerheads clustered onto 30-inch (76cm) stems. Silver-grey *E. giganteum* is a biennial plant, also known as 'Miss Willmott's Ghost'. *E. maritimum*, the native sea-holly of sandy shores and dunes, bears spectacular blue-green spiny ruffs around dense heads of flowers and foliage. All of them do well in a sunny position in well-drained and light soils, and are great for seaside gardens. As they grow on taproots, they resent being moved about, but in spring or autumn young plants can be planted out where they are intended to flower.

Angelica

Imposing foliage and magnificent domed flowerheads borne on strong, 6-foot (2m) tall stems, make *Angelica archangelica* a very ornamental plant. Its archaic name, *Herba angelica*, derives from the story that its medicinal properties were revealed to a monk by an angel. It was used as an antidote to poisons and plague, as an aphrodisiac, and to protect against witches, – clearly a plant of multiple virtues.

In the garden, this hardy biennial thrives in moist, fertile soil, preferably where it will receive a little shade for part of the day. *Angelica* must be grown from seed, sown as freshly as possible; plants produce a rosette of foliage in the first year, out of which rise the flowering stems in the second year. It self-sows freely, and the seedlings can be transplanted to their final flowering positions in autumn.

August

For those of us that cannot get away on holiday, August brings the compensation of late-season flowers, harvests of home-grown salads and fruits, and certainly a chance for some outdoor armchair gardening. It is generally a quiet time in the garden, with little to do that is urgent except harvesting and routine tidying. It is, however, a good time to revise planting plans, order more bulbs, and note changes that can be carried out next month.

ORNAMENTAL GARDEN

Trimming & Dead-heading

Remove spent flowerheads that are turning brown on buddleia. New flowers for the coming weeks will emerge from shoots further down the stems.

Dead-head sisyrinchiums when the flowers are spent (leaving some old flowerheads intact if you want seeds, which will self-sow around the garden).

Wisteria
Finish summer pruning of wisterias. It isn't worth saving seed from the long, bean-like pods that develop because the wisteria you can raise from seed are nearly always inferior to the grafted varieties sold by nurseries, and will often take many years to begin flowering.

Rambler roses
Old flowering shoots of rambler roses should be cut out close to the ground, and new branches tied in to replace the old. Thick branches can be taken out with a sharp pruning saw or strong loppers.

Bushy herbs
Using shears, trim shoot tops and spent flowerheads on santolinas, curry plants and lavender.

Hedges and Topiaries
In order to improve accuracy when trimming formal hedges, follow a guideline of string pulled taut at the desired height, and use hand-shears (not powered trimmers) for the soft growth on the hedge-top. Electric or battery-powered hedge-trimmers make quick work of the sides: work from

the bottom of the hedge upwards, as trimmings are then less likely to be caught up in the foliage. When reshaping hedges, make the bottom wider in section than the top so that light can reach the lowest branches and keep them furnished in leaves.

New Plants

Seed harvest

Collect ripened seeds of aquilegias, alliums, poppies, and other early summer flowers, then clean them thoroughly by removing seed capsules and other debris. To keep them fresh until sowing time, store them in manilla 'wages' envelopes in the refrigerator.

Annuals

Rather than hoping that poorly performing annuals and bedding plants will recover, replace them with new stock – either leftover plants growing on in pots for emergencies, or late-season bargains at garden centres.

Bulbs

As a guideline, daffodils should be planted at three times their own depth; for largish bulbs, special bulb-planters make the job quicker as they pull out a plug of soil to the right depth. Bulbs should be planted as soon as you buy them; but if delay is un-

Quick Tip
Chopped-up banana skins spread around rose bushes make good fertiliser and help discourage greenfly. *E Bleech*

avoidable, you can keep them healthy by storing them in fresh, damp coir-fibre in a dark place.

Plant out rock-garden bulbs such as crocuses, *Reticulata* irises, dwarf narcissi and muscari. These dwarf bulbs are also suitable for outdoor containers filled with free-draining, gritty compost.

Cuttings

Take heel cuttings of box plants. Dense, dwarf box (*Buxus sempervirens* 'Suffruticosa') takes ages to grow, but you can get decent-sized plants more quickly from small branches, with several leaf stems attached, pulled from the middle of the bush. Plant out into a nursery bed of gritty soil, or pot up in a 50:50 mix of grit and soil-based potting compost.

Choice asters

Flowers with ethereal mauvey-blue tones are especially uplifting at this time of year, particularly in the fading light of early evening. Look out for *Aster macrophyllus* 'Twilight' – elegant and prolific blue daisies with a silvery sheen (30 inches/76cm tall), the shorter *A. thomsonii* 'Nanus' (2 feet/60cm), and the mutable *Phlox paniculata* 'Blue Paradise' (30–40 inches/76–100cm).

Container Feeds

To prolong flowering displays, continue feeding all seasonal plants grown in pots with a weak solution of liquid fertiliser applied weekly, and dead-head spent flowers so the plants' energy is not diverted into seed production.

Pests

Ants

Treat ants' nests in lawns and in cracks in paving. If you don't like using ant powders, a rapid and chemical-free way of dealing with them is to pour a kettleful of boiling water over the nest.

Lacewing allies

The larvae of lacewings are valuable garden allies, being voracious eaters of aphids. The 'lacewing chamber' (with lacewing attractant) is designed to provide the ideal shelter that the creatures seek in late summer and early autumn. The chamber is available from Biotal (tel. 01634 262216), and some garden centres. It should be set up later this month, and moved to a shed or garage in November for overwintering.

KITCHEN GARDEN

Weeds

Run a hoe between rows of vegetables to uproot weed seedlings.

New Crops

Salads

Sow late salad crops of lettuce, radishes, spring onions, and wild rocket. 'Rossa di Treviso' – an old, deep-red, hardy radicchio from Italy – can be sown now for late-winter and early-spring harvests.

Parsley
Sow parsley to be grown on under cloches when cooler weather arrives.

Onions
Buy onion sets, such as yellow-skinned 'Pesto' and red-onion 'Romy', for autumn planting.

Strawberries
Plant new strawberries from certified healthy stock, setting them out 18 inches (46cm) apart. Plant firmly, ensuring the crown is exactly at soil level. Water well and ensure plants do not dry out.

Care & Maintenance

Sweetcorn
Harvest sweetcorn when the cobs lean away from the stalks and the silks are brown and withered.

Cucurbits
Lift marrows, squashes and pumpkins clear of the ground and rest them on timber or dry newspaper while they ripen.

Tomatoes
Pinch out the tops of outdoor tomatoes when three trusses of fruit have developed, and continue to remove side-shoots (except on bush tomatoes).

Fruit
Provide support for heavily laden branches of plums as the brittle branches can easily break off.

Prune summer-fruiting raspberries: cut down the old fruited canes and tie in new ones.

Composting

Rather than burning healthy soft material from late-season prunings, add them to the compost heap. A compost accelerator (such as Biotal) will significantly help the decomposing process. There are special formulae for breaking down leaves or grass mowings, as well as general mixed waste.

Pests

Protect fruit trees from winter moths: the wingless females climb tree trunks in autumn to lay eggs, and the resulting caterpillars cause damage. Grease-bands and paint-on barrier grease for fruit trees will prevent them reaching their target. If you keep grease-bands on fruit trees through the year, check now to see if they need renewing.

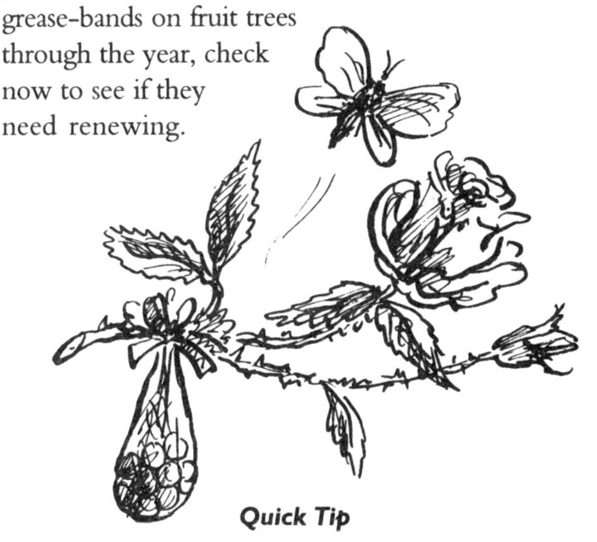

Quick Tip

To prevent birds from pecking fruit on trees, tie a bag of mothballs to the lowest branch.

Mrs Margaret Rooke

INDOORS & UNDER GLASS

Houseplants

Before you go away on holiday, give houseplants a thorough watering, then move them away from hot, sunny windowsills and group them together in a shady position. Trays of wet gravel, or dampened capillary matting on the draining board or in the bath, will provide them with enough moisture to last a couple of weeks.

Pot on any pot-bound house and conservatory plants. If leaves are looking pale and mottled, check them for red spider-mite infestations *(see* June). Increase humidity around affected plants by misting regularly with a fine water spray and standing pots on trays of wet gravel.

Indoor bulbs

Plant 'Paper White' narcissi for winter indoor displays. For bowls without drainage holes proprietary bulb-fibre is best as it helps root growth and soil aeration; otherwise, any good potting compost is suitable. Plant bulbs close together, with the tips just showing on the surface. Keep in a dark, cool place for eight to twelve weeks while the roots develop.

QUESTIONS & ANSWERS

My new flat, on the south coast, has a sunny balcony with plenty of space for potted plants. What would be suitable to grow on it?

Mrs B Chamberlain, Brighton

Choose plants that are tolerant of wind and salt-laden air. For evergreenery, try *Phillyrea*, *Escallonia*,

Olearia, or bay. Yuccas and phormiums, which have very sculptural, sword-shaped foliage, are also good evergreens. In the mild climate, colourful geraniums (pelargoniums) may flower all the year round. For summer colour, add osteospermums, *Caryopteris, Erigeron, Mesembryanthemum, Kniphofia*, or *Agapanthus*. Use a soil-based John Innes compost, and feed and water regularly.

ﬤ

A beautiful tree at the bottom of next-door's garden gives us privacy from houses that back onto ours. I'd hate anyone to cut it down, and I have heard that you can get protection orders put on almost any tree. Is that right?

M R Reed, Bromley

You refer to a 'tree preservation order', which can be granted only by the local planning authority under the Town and Country Planning Act of 1980. It's often used to protect trees under threat on sites up for development. It may not be so easy to get an order for your neighbour's tree – unless they are threatening to chop it down – because it is on their property. However, it might be as well to tell them how much you appreciate it!

ﬤ

The hydrangea I have been growing in a pot since last year, has not flowered at all this summer. What could be wrong?

Joan Collins, Northampton

There are several possibilities: you may need to pot it on into a larger pot, or preferably a big tub, with fresh potting soil; do remember to water and feed it regularly. It might be in too shady a position for its stems to develop good flowerbuds. Or it may have been pruned too hard. Ensure it is in a bright position, and prune it only lightly at the tips, in April. You should get good flowers next year.

Looking Good in August ...

Purple cone-flower

You might know of the mauve cone-flower, *Echinacea purpurea*, as a health food supplement. This hardy perennial (which has been used medicinally for centuries by Native Americans) reaches 4 feet (120cm) or more. It's great from high summer into autumn, when it bears large daisy flowers of a brilliant pinky-mauve hue, with a rust-brown central cone that darkens with age. Plant it in fertile soil in an open, sunny position, and dead-head regularly. Propagate in early spring by dividing the rootstock or potting up root-cuttings to grow on under glass. 'White Lustre' and 'White Swan' are paler-petalled alternatives.

African lilies

Agapanthus, the African lily, deserves pride of place this month. Many of these fleshy-rooted perennials are completely hardy when grown on freely draining soil in a sunny spot – generally, those with the narrowest leaves are the hardiest. Pretty varieties include the 'Headbourne Hybrids', the deep-indigo 'Bressingham Blue', and the diminutive 'Lilliput'. African lilies also make striking pot-plants, although they may take a couple of years to build up enough steam to flower, which they only do well once their roots have filled the pot. Try them in bright, galvanised florists' buckets for a contemporary look, but be sure to bring them under glass for winter protection.

September

September's weather can be some of the nicest of the year; better still it brings with it the rich hues and fruitfulness of the autumn season: conkers and chestnuts bursting from their shells and keeping squirrels busy; rosy apples and pears complementing the vibrant colours of cosmos, cleome, tobacco flower and tree mallow, salvias and perovskias; and flowering grasses fluttering in the lightest breeze.

ORNAMENTAL GARDEN

New Plants

Lawns

Sow new lawns and reseed patches in existing turf. Buy fresh, good-quality seed from a reputable supplier, and choose a mixture suitable for the sort of wear that the lawn will receive. Sow into well-prepared, weed-free ground, and keep it watered regularly, particularly if the autumn is dry.

New trees and shrubs
This is an ideal time to plant out container-grown trees and shrubs. Choose healthy-looking stock, rejecting any plants that appear starved, under-watered or have weeds growing in the container. Provide stake supports for trees where required, and water regularly.

Siberian iris
Lift and divide clumps of Siberian iris. These versatile plants are suited to good soil in flower borders as well as the permanently moist soil of a bog-garden or poolside.

Wildflower bulbs
John Shipton Bulbs (tel. 01994 240125), a specialist producer of British native bulbs from reputable sources, can supply cultivated stock of *Narcissus pseudonarcissus* (the daffodil immortalised by Wordsworth), its subspecies *obvallaris* (the

Quick Tip

Children's windmills make very effective squirrel deterrents. *Christopher A McIntyre*

Tenby daffodil), plus squills, snowflakes, anemones, and much else suitable for naturalising.

New clematis
Plant clematis and other new climbers into well-prepared ground.

Care & Maintenenance

September is a good month to carry out construction work in the garden, while days are still fairly long, and comparatively warm.

Lawns
Scarify the lawn to remove dead grass (thatch) and so allow more light and air to reach the roots. For large lawns, motorised lawn-rakers make the job easier; small lawns can be done by hand with a spring-tined rake. Rake strongly in each direction, then use a besom or plastic rake to gather the thatch (which can be composted). A well-scarified lawn yields a surprisingly large amount of debris.

Pond protection
Put wire mesh or netting over ponds to prevent falling leaves from fouling the water.

Tidying borders
Clear away scruffy remains of herbaceous plants that have finished contributing anything this year. Tidy up borders and remove seedling weeds.

Pests

Weevil action
This month is the last chance this year to use vine-weevil nematodes (other than in heated

areas indoors). They need to be watered in while soil temperatures are still warm.

KITCHEN GARDEN

Fruit

Prune out old raspberry canes by cutting back to ground level and destroying the prunings; they are not worth shredding and composting as they can be a source of disease. Tie down this year's new canes that will provide next summer's fruit.

Wasps

Wasps are generally useful creatures, with a good appetite for aphids, but if they are interfering with ripening fruit you may want to reduce their numbers by making a trap for them: put some beer or jam in a jam-jar, and fasten a paper lid, with a small hole in it, over the top.

At this time of year, keep some neat tea-tree oil to hand; it relieves wasp stings instantly.

Vegetable Crops

Root vegetables

Towards the end of the month, lift and store root vegetables for winter use. Only those in perfect condition should be stored, in layers between fresh coir-fibre. Brand-new metal dustbins with close-fitting lids make ideal, rodent-resistant storage containers for a cool shed or garage.

Cabbages

Sow pointed spring cabbage such as 'Durham Early' directly where it is to mature, thinning out resulting seedlings to 10 inches (25cm) apart.

Asparagus
Cut asparagus ferns to the ground and burn them as they may be harbouring overwintering eggs of the asparagus beetle. Apply a balanced feed, such as blood, fish and bonemeal, over the soil surface.

Prepare new asparagus beds for planting out crowns next spring: remove weeds and dig in plenty of well-rotted compost or manure.

Herbs

Lift and divide hardy perennial herbs, replanting the most vigorous sections of root. Calamints, lemon balm, lovage, mint, chives, salad burnet and betony are suitable for this treatment.

Composting

Start a new compost heap to take this autumn's (compostable) prunings and fallen leaves.

INDOORS & UNDER GLASS

Reduce watering of succulents and cacti, and provide current-season flowering plants with a liquid feed; remove any debris and dead foliage.

❋ *Quick Tips* ❋

Grow nasturtiums around the base of apple trees to prevent aphids attacking the tree and its fruit. *D Chandler*

Over-ripe tomatoes will become firm if they are placed in a basin of salted water for about 20 minutes. *Reg Davies*

Adding manure to the compost heap will help the compost to 'cook' more quickly. *Mrs D Clarke*

New Plants from Old

There is still time to take cuttings from half-hardy plants such as *Osteospermum*, *Argyranthemum*, many salvias, *Penstemon*, *Bidens*, *Pelargonium*, and *Verbena*. Place several cuttings (1½–2½ inches/4–6.5cm long) in a pot, in half and half John Innes compost and vermiculite (or grit). Place on a windowsill or greenhouse bench where they will receive gentle warmth and sunlight.

Lavatera

Take semi-ripe cuttings (3–4 inch/8–10cm long shoots with a heel of bark attached) and dip in rooting powder; pot up in gritty compost, and keep in a shaded cold-frame or cool greenhouse.

Seeds

New primulas

Sow seeds of polyanthus and auriculas in a cool greenhouse, in John Innes seed compost.

Hot-water plant

Sow seeds of schizanthus, the 'hot-water plant', to grow as pot-plants for warm greenhouse or conservatory displays next spring.

Sweet-peas

For early flowers next year, order sweet-pea seeds for sowing under glass next month. Unwins (tel.

❋ ***Quick Tips*** ❋

Old clothes (of natural fibres only) such as woollen jumpers can be chopped up and added to the compost heap. *Miss J White*

01945 588522) offers a good range of extra fragrant varieties in separate colours.

Potted Bulbs

Plant up small spring bulbs, such as species crocuses, *Reticulata* irises, *Scilla*, *Muscari* and *Chionodoxa*, quite closely together into small pots or shallow 'alpine' pans of free-draining, gritty compost. Traditional clay alpine pans are obtainable from Willow Pottery, Bath (tel. 01225 859902).

Houseplants

Bring indoors any houseplants that have been enjoying a spell outside. Some may need repotting into fresh compost, but in any case check them closely for signs of pest attack.

QUESTIONS & ANSWERS

Our new home has scores of rabbits in the large garden. Will we ever be able to grow anything?

A Gilbert, Tonbridge

Anything you grow will certainly need a physical barrier to protect it. Work out your priorities and section off the areas that you intend to cultivate first – a kitchen, or flower, garden, perhaps.

Make a rabbit-proof fence of galvanised wire netting, at least 3 feet (90cm) high. At least 1 foot (30cm) of it should be buried underground (including the ground beneath any gate), tilted outwards to prevent the rabbits burrowing under it. Individual trees can be protected with tree-guards (peruse the small ads in gardening magazines for suppliers).

In my experience, it helps if you have an agile cat or two prowling around – they will soon get the problem under control.

Toadstools are appearing on the lawn and, while I have no great quarrel with them (they are not unattractive), I worry that they are harming the grass, or perhaps the plants near by.

R Vickers, Hornchurch

Toadstools often appear on lawns in the autumn, and in mild, damp periods, but their presence is usually fleeting because the arrival of frost kills them off. They feed on organic matter in the soil, and usually do no harm to grass.

Circular fungus patterns known as fairy-rings are more damaging, but there is no chemical treatment

available to gardeners and, unless you are prepared to dig out and replace the affected and nearby turf, and the soil beneath it (to a depth of 1 foot/30cm), it is better to live with them. To keep them under control, sweep them away when they appear (before their caps open to release more spores).

Looking Good in September

Gaura lindheimeri

From slender pink buds, the starry white flowers of *Gaura lindheimeri* burst open along tall, wiry stems. This clump-forming perennial from Texas and Louisiana has delicate blooms that flutter like pale butterflies in the breeze. It enjoys a warm, sunny position and freely draining soil. Being rather lax in habit, its slender stems (3–4 feet/1–1.2m tall) benefit from the support of discreetly placed pea-sticks, or sturdier neighbouring plants, such as lavender and *Sisyrinchium striatum*. It also looks wonderful growing among ornamental grasses.

Japanese anemones

Of all the plants that flower in autumn to herald the coming of winter, few can be quite as welcome as the hardy, perennial, Japanese anemone (*Anemone* x *hybrida* and others). When open, its pink or white flowers, on 3–5 foot (1–1.5m) stems, rather resembles its close relation, the buttercup. The best white forms include 'Honorine Jobert' and the vigorous, semi-double cultivar 'Luise Uhink'. Of the pink shades, look out for 'Queen Charlotte' (semi-double), and deep-rose 'Pamina' and 'Hadspen Abundance' – all of them absolutely gorgeous.

They are generally trouble-free, and enjoy a sunny or partially shaded position with good, fertile soil. Large plants can be lifted and divided in early spring.

❋ TOPIARY

Topiary – the gentle art of training and clipping – has become fashionable recently; but the art is an enduring one, for the techniques go back at least two thousand years when the Romans created living-plant structures for their gardens.

From spring to autumn, topiary provides a calm, green foil for the vivid colour of the herbaceous flowers; in winter, it can be a valuable way of bringing evergreen structure and sculpture into the garden in either a formal or a light-hearted way. At any time of year, topiary can be used to create eye-catching focal points.

Topiary isn't instant (unless you cheat and buy it ready-made): it takes three to five years to get a good outline established. The thing that usually puts people off, though, is the assumption that it is difficult. But that isn't really true. Geometric shapes, such as balls, cones, pyramids and cubes, are quite easy; you can do it freehand if you have a fairly good eye, otherwise it is best to buy or make a template to cut around. Start with small plants of privet or box, and use sharp shears or secateurs.

Cottage-garden topiary often features animals – usually birds and cats – or tiered 'cake-stand' shapes. Usually, the tree (a young yew, or box bush) will have suggested a shape, which the topiarist then decided to exploit by, for example, tying some branches one way to form a tail, and some the other way for a head. Some trees and shrubs are especially suitable for topiary, Hawthorn, although deciduous, makes good large topiary, and the dense, slow-growing Japanese holly (*Ilex crenata*), small-leaved (rather like box), is also very good.

Making topiary is rather like cutting hair, but more fun. Don't worry if it doesn't shape up quite as you planned: the shoots will grow back again and you can have another go next year!

October

Through October, keen gardeners are like jugglers as they struggle to keep all the balls in the air: pruning and harvesting; seed-saving and leaf-sweeping; digging up and dividing border plants, and perhaps planting new ones. Depending on where you live and how the season shapes up, you may have some late but balmy sunshine (it won't last, so make the most of it) or dark days of rain and gloomy skies; usually, there's a bit of each. The season's dampness and its abundant leaf-fall means it is a good time to start a compost heap, or at least a leaf-heap. Never burn autumn's leaves: they can be turned into a rich soil conditioner in a matter of months, simply by stacking them up and leaving well alone.

ORNAMENTAL GARDEN

Remove the last remaining summer bedding plants from beds and containers. Annuals should

be composted or discarded, but sometimes it can be worth saving marguerites (*Argyranthemum*), pelargoniums, perennial nemesias and osteospermums. Keep them in a light position in a frost-free greenhouse or conservatory.

New Plants

New biennials
Finish planting out biennials where they are required to flower next year.

New roses
For the best choice of roses, now is the time to order bare-rooted ones, from the catalogues of specialist nurseries, for planting out this winter.

New hedges
Plant new hedges, trees and shrubs firmly into well-prepared holes. When planting trees, remember to ram stakes firmly into the ground *before* the tree goes in to avoid damaging the roots with it. Use adjustable tree-ties to join stake and tree.

Next year's bulbs
Finish planting spring bulbs in the ground and in containers. Plant tulip bulbs late – towards the end of the month, or even during November – as this reduces the risk of their being exposed to soil-borne diseases, to which tulips are prone.

Seed saving
Continue collecting and drying seeds, and dead-heading late flowers where seeds are not required.

Preparing for Winter

Finish trimming evergreen hedges, and shorten long, trailing stems on shrub roses to reduce rocking in high winds.

Mulching
Lay a 2–3 inch (5–8cm) thick mulch around shrubs. Composted bark, manure, garden or mush-room compost are good general mulches. Cocoa shells (left over from chocolate production and sold in garden centres) slightly acidify the soil, so they are especially useful for mulching pieris, rhododendrons, camellias and other ericaceous shrubs.

Thinning out perennials
This is the perfect time to lift and divide herbaceous perennials. Once lifted, ensure the roots are not left lying around exposed for any length of time as they quickly dry out. Spray them with a little water, and keep them in plastic bags or covered with polythene sheeting while you replenish the soil with well-rotted compost (mixed with plenty of coarse grit if the soil is heavy clay) before replanting them.

Dahlias
Cut off the old flowered stems of dahlias and lift out the tubers. Store the tubers in an airy, dark and dry place for replanting next year.

Alpines
Provide each of your alpines with a wide collar of grit to protect vulnerable plants from too much autumn wetness.

Lawns

While grass is still growing, continue mowing the lawn as required, but with the blades set quite high. During frost-free weather, carry out new turfing jobs and lawn repairs.

Worm casts
Worm casts are a nuisance when trodden into the grass as they become ideal seedbeds for weeds. But the soil processed by worms is fine and nutritious, and there is the added consolation that the worms are aerating the lawn for you. During dry weather you can break the casts and disperse them by beating the lawn with a besom broom so that the fine, scattered soil that makes up the casts can be washed back into the ground. Alternatively, pick up and remove the casts to flower or vegetable beds.

Autumn Leaves

Continue gathering fallen leaves regularly. If you haven't a compost heap, put damp leaves into black plastic bin-liner bags, which can be stored out of sight for the next eight to twelve months. The rotted-down leaf-mould that results makes an excellent mulch.

Make a separate compost heap for really tough leaves, such as beech, oak and plane, which take ages to rot down. Shredding or mowing the leaves helps to break them down a little before composting, and garden centres sell compost activators specially blended to assist the rotting process of leaves.

KITCHEN GARDEN

Fruit

October is all about fruit: choosing, ordering, planting, harvesting, eating. Prepare the soil for new fruit trees and bushes, ensuring heavy soils have adequate drainage. Work plenty of well-rotted compost into each planting position, and add a slow-release general fertiliser at planting time.

Storage

Store surplus ripe apples if you have somewhere sufficiently cool, dark and mouse-free. Only perfect fruit should be stored; any that is bruised and damaged can be pressed for juice, which can then be frozen. Vigo Vineyard Supplies (tel. 01823 680230) sells a range of sturdy traditional fruit-presses and crushers.

❋ *Quick Tips* ❋

Shake a Cox's apple before you eat it. It is ripe and ready if you can hear the pips rattling inside. *Mrs Jenny Brown*

Nasturtiums grown around the base of apple trees will discourage aphids from attacking the tree and its fruit. *D Chandler*

Unusual fruit

Now is the time to plant a quince. This attractive small tree (*Cydonia oblonga*, not to be confused with *Chaenomeles japonica* varieties popularly sold as quinces in garden centres), has large flowers like apple blossom in spring, and fragrant, golden, pear-shaped fruits in autumn; just one fruit will perfume a whole room. They are undemanding trees, but grow best in southern counties, in good soil and a sunny, open position. Two popular varieties are 'Meech's Prolific' and 'Vranja'. Fruit specialists Reads Nursery in Norfolk (tel. 01508 548395) and Deacon's Nursery on the Isle of Wight (tel. 01983 840750) do mail order.

Quick Tip

Attach a rope to a child's skateboard: it makes an ideal trolley for shifting heavy objects around the garden. *Mrs P Phelan*

Peach protection
Bordeaux mixture (a copper-based fungicide containing finely ground slaked lime and copper sulphate) is an approved organic method of reducing the damaging effects of peach-leaf curl disease on outdoor peaches, nectarines and almond trees. Spray now to kill fungal spores before they settle into bark crevices and dormant buds for the winter. Cover wall-trained trees with open-sided polythene to prevent rain washing spores into the buds.

Vegetables

Start digging and manuring redundant areas of the vegetable garden.

Jerusalem artichokes
Cut down canes of Jerusalem artichokes to about 1 foot (30cm) above the ground. Leave the tubers where they are, and dig them out as required over the coming months.

Broad beans
Sow 'Aquadulce Claudia' broad beans now for an early crop next year. Place seeds 8 inches (20cm) apart and 2 inches (5cm) deep. (Suppliers include Thompson & Morgan, tel. 01473 690869 and Marshalls, tel. 01945 466711).

INDOORS & UNDER GLASS

Keep the greenhouse well-ventilated in the day, and carry out watering early each day so that plants are not damp on cold nights. Check now that greenhouse heaters are in good working order, and ensure that greenhouse work surfaces and window panes are clean. Put up insulation (rolls of bubble-wrap polythene can be bought by mail or from garden centres), and cover the vents separately so they can be opened independently as needed.

Sowing & Potting

Early sweet-peas
For earlier flowering sweet-peas next year, sow them now, half an inch (1.5cm) deep into 5-inch (13cm) pots, several seeds per pot, in ordinary seed compost. Cover with glass or polythene until seedlings break through the compost surface. These hardy annuals benefit from the winter shelter of a cold greenhouse or frame, and should be kept very cool and light to prevent straggly, weak growth.

More mint
Pot up some roots of mint for growing under glass, to extend its season into the winter.

QUESTIONS & ANSWERS

Various toadstools – and possibly mushrooms – grow in our garden and the woods beyond. I've tried to look them up in books but am reluctant to harvest any for eating in case they're poisonous. How can we be sure which ones are safe?

M Sheppard, Chesterfield

You're right to be wary; it takes a very skilled eye to distinguish the edible from the inedible, and it is never wise to take chances. The best way to learn about wild fungi is to take one of the excellent courses run by the Field Studies Council, Preston

Montford, Montford Bridge, Shrewsbury SY4 1HW (tel. 01743 850674). They have a range of courses (including residential weekends) at fungi-rich locations countrywide, all offering expert advice to beginners on what you can and can't eat, and which fungi are truly delicious.

ꝭ

My wife and I want to plant a 'silver' border in the garden to commemorate our silver wedding anniversary. Is this practical, and what plants should we choose?

M Brooke, Blandford

It's a lovely idea, and easy to do. Many 'silver' (or, strictly speaking, grey-leaved) plants come from arid lands, so choose a bright, sunny position with freely draining soil. You could build up a tapestry of *Stachys byzantina* (lamb's ears), artemisias, such as 'Powis Castle', lavenders, *Convolvulus cneorum*, *Santolina incana*, and steely eryngiums. Add height and contrasting hues to enhance the silvers with marble-leaved rosettes of *Silybum marianum*, buddleias, clary sage (*Salvia sclarea* var. turkestanica), 'Bowles Mauve' wallflowers, and purple orache.

Looking Good in October ...

Salvia involucrata

Many salvias will keep colour in the garden well into autumn. One of the most dramatic is *Salvia involucrata*, a 5–6 foot (1.5–1.8m) tall Mexican species whose spikes of lipstick-like flowers in brilliant magenta positively dazzle. Its large, soft-green leaves have deep-pink veins while the stems are suffused with deeper purple.

It's reasonably hardy in the shelter of a south- or west-facing wall in well-drained soil; in cold areas it can also be grown as a conservatory plant. In winter it dies back, so treat it as a herbaceous perennial and cut down the previous year's flower stems in spring. Propagate by cuttings taken in summer.

Persian ironwood tree

The Persian ironwood tree, *Parrotia persica*, is one of the most distinctive of autumn's foliage plants. As the colder weather sets in, its tough, beech-like leaves turn rich crimson and gold. Usually, it grows on a fairly short trunk, and throws out wide-spreading branches, which gives it a broad, squat appearance.

Grow *Parrotia* in an open sunny position for best foliage colour, and on fertile but well-drained loamy soil (slightly acidic soil yields the richest tints). Early spring bulbs, such as *Crocus tommasinianus*, *Cyclamen corum* and snowdrops can be grown beneath it, and will have passed their moment of glory well before the tree's new leaves emerge. It can grow up to 20 feet (6m) high and 25 feet (7.5m) across, but it takes about twenty years to reach even half that size.

November

Though the rich autumn colours are still with us in early November, the daylight hours are noticeably decreasing, and tender plants must be protected as the colder weather sets in. Some of them, such as tulbaghias and salvias – and pelargoniums on the windowsill – may still be flowering their heads off. Should you cut it all down and be rid of last season's leftovers? Or continue to enjoy them while they last? The latter, I think, don't you? For at this stage of the year, spring seems a long way off.

ORNAMENTAL GARDEN

In between clearing and composting fallen leaves, clean and put away patio pots that are not to be used for winter plantings. During mild weather, lay a mulch of garden compost or well-rotted manure over beds that have been cut back and tidied.

Shrubs, Trees & Hedges

Provided that the ground is not frozen or waterlogged, plant bare-rooted roses, shrubs and trees bought from specialist nurseries. Dig a substantial hole for each plant, and work in well-rotted manure or compost, with some slow-release general fertiliser or bonemeal to aid root establishment. Soaking the roots for an hour or so in a solution of Maxicrop organic seaweed fertiliser immediately before planting is also beneficial. Ensure plants are set firmly in the ground at their original soil level. If rabbits or deer are a problem, fit protective tree-shelters at the same time.

Later in the month, tread the soil firmly around recently planted trees and shrubs whose roots may have been loosened in high winds.

This is also prime time for planting deciduous hedges, such as hornbeam, beech, field maple and hawthorn. These, and various mixtures of native hedgerow plants, are available by the yard from Buckingham Nurseries (tel. 01280 813556).

New Plants

Perennials

Continue dividing and replanting herbaceous perennials. And plant out pot-grown hellebores for their wonderful flowers in late winter and spring.

Bulbs and Tubers

If you see healthy lily bulbs for sale, buy and plant them now, rather than in spring. The extra time they'll have to get established will mean better quality flowers next year. Plant in good, rich, freely draining soil to which organic matter (such as garden compost) has been added. Most lilies like deep planting (5–8 inches/12.5–20cm). Slightly dry-looking bulbs should be revived in buckets of damp coir-fibre for a couple of days before planting. Purple *Lilium martagon* (Turk's-cap lily) is good for naturalising in rough grass among deciduous trees. Plant them just 4 inches (11cm) deep.

Plant tulips now, too, well down in deep pots of soil-based (John Innes-type) compost.

Cut down remaining stems from dahlias, and lift and store the tubers.

Cuttings

Take hardwood cuttings of favourite shrubs including roses, *Philadelphus*, *Deutzia*, *Forsythia* and *Ribes*.

Plant labels

Replenish plant labels now, while you can still remember which plants are where. And set labels into the ground where new bulbs have been planted.

Pruning

Hard-prune overgrown deciduous hedges, using a pruning saw or loppers to cut through thick stems. (ARS saws from Burton McCall are very good; tel. 01162 340800 for nearest stockists.) Extremely overgrown hedges should be renovated: to limit shock to the plants, cut the top and only one side hard back; prune the other side next year. After trimming, feed with a slow-release, phosphorous-rich fertiliser, such as sterilised bonemeal.

❋ *Quick Tip* ❋

To keep a plastic bag open for garden rubbish, line it with a cardboard box with the bottom knocked out. *W Bowen Davies*

Lawns

To save time in spring, sharpen up lawn edges now with a flat, half-moon iron designed for the job (garden spades are unsuitable as their curved blade can create a scalloped effect). Repair worn patches, laying new turves as soon as they arrive: cut out the old sections of turf, lightly fork over the soil underneath, and add some sharp sand to help aerate the soil. Dress the soil surface with blood, fish and bone mixture or general slow-release fertiliser. Lay new turf, firming it down gently and ensuring the new surface is level with the old.

Winter Protection

Protect plants vulnerable to cold with cloches. The 10-inch (25cm) high Solar Bell (made from recycled plastic) and the 14-inch (35cm) high Big Bell, are available from Haxnicks (tel. 01747 870296).

Pipes
Wrap all outdoor pipes and taps with protective lagging to help prevent them from freezing up. Drain off and store hosepipes, and bring automatic watering timers indoors.

Holly Berries

If the birds always eat all the holly berries before you get a chance to use them at Christmas, cut some berried branches at the end of this month, and store them in a cool, bright place (a cold frame, or under polythene in a greenhouse is ideal), where they will not lose too much moisture.

KITCHEN GARDEN

On heavy soils, continue digging over vacant areas of the vegetable garden, incorporating manure or garden compost into the soil as you work.

Provide cloche cover for salad herbs such as parsley and chervil, and put netting or fine fleece over sprouts and cabbages to protect them from birds.

Preparing for Spring

Storage

Take down the temporary structures that supported runner beans, sweet-peas, etc. Clean the canes before storing them somewhere dry.

Blackcurrants

Prune blackcurrant bushes, taking out the oldest branches (those that are three years old or more), at the base. Select a few healthy 10-inch (25cm) long shoots of this year's growth for hardwood cuttings.

Next year's seeds

Order seeds from the new catalogues now. Suppliers of a broad range of flowers and vegetables include Thompson & Morgan (tel. 01473 688821), E W King (tel. 01376 570000) Suttons (tel. 01803 614614), D T Brown (freephone 0800 7311231), and Marshalls (who specialise in the kitchen garden, tel. 01945 466711). For organic seeds, try Ferme de Sainte Marthe (tel. 01932 266630), Chase Organics (tel. 01932 253666), or Suffolk Herbs (tel. 01376 572456).

Fruit Check

Check fruits in store, and discard any that are showing signs of decay.

INDOORS & UNDER GLASS

New Plants

Winter lettuce

Sow winter-tolerant lettuces in clean soil in a cold-frame or cold or slightly heated greenhouse. 'Winter Density', from DT Brown (tel. 01253 882371), 'Lianne' and 'Lobjoits Green Cos' from Suttons (tel. 01803 614614), are suitable.

African violets

Take leaf-cuttings of African violets by using a sharp knife to cut off a healthy, full-sized leaf as close to the stalk base as possible. Trim the leaf stalk to about 1½ inches (8cm) long, and insert 1 inch (2.5cm) of it into ordinary potting compost mixed half-and-half with vermiculite to improve drainage.

Overwintering Plants

Be selective when watering greenhouse and indoor plants from now on. With the reduced light and temperatures of the season, many plants' water requirements are much reduced. To prevent mossy growth developing on the compost surface of potted plants, dress with a layer of coarse grit; to prevent the build up of disease, remove dead leaves as they occur.

Ensure that the greenhouse is well ventilated during periods of bright sunshine, but close vents during cold or wet weather.

Cyclamen

Place potted cyclamen in a cool, bright position to reduce the likelihood of yellowing leaves and elongated flower-stalks. Always apply water to the base of the plant, never into the top of the pot.

Fuchsias

Keep tender fuchsias in a frost-free greenhouse or conservatory, and regularly remove dead leaves to prevent the development of disease. Flowering may continue in warm conditions; if not, keep the compost of dormant plants almost dry.

❋ *Quick Tips* ❋

To protect slightly tender plants from frost and snow, cover with the clippings from coniferous plants. *Heather Owen*

Bury grass-clippings, soft prunings and vegetable rubbish (but not weeds) around the garden. The worms will do the work, saving the need for an unsightly compost heap. *Linda Thompson*

QUESTIONS & ANSWERS

One of the main branches of our Robinia *'Frisia' tree was blown down in a gale. Is the tree ruined for life?*

Mrs J Rice, London

Robinias have fairly inflexible, brittle branches, so they are prone to breaking off in gales. However, these trees do have remarkable powers of regeneration so it is most likely that it will make a good recovery. It may be worth getting a tree surgeon to neaten up the wound and check the tree for any other signs of damage.

℘

I brought a couple of lemon trees indoors this September to display in the hall but they are not doing too well. Where would be the best place for them?

Mrs D Rhodes, Alresford

Citrus plants need somewhere warm – at least 50°F (10°C), but away from hot radiators – and with as much light as possible. So, unless it's draught-free and very bright indeed, your hall is not ideal, and your plants would be better near a window or French windows. Water only when the top of the compost becomes dry, and your plants should be ready for repotting into a slightly larger pot next spring.

Looking Good in November ...

Ginkgo, the maidenhair tree

The maidenhair tree, *Ginkgo biloba*, is one of the oldest plants on Earth. It existed in the dinosaur age and has been revered in the Far East for hundreds of years as a herbal remedy for poor blood circulation. Its leaves, which resemble open fans, with rippled, notched edges, are lime-green in summer, but in autumn turn a vivid, glowing yellow (of a particularly vibrant hue after a hot summer). Its distinctive branches have a knobbly, irregular appearance. Although potentially a large tree in old age, its growth is moderate and not very widely spreading, so it makes a good feature tree in small, or urban gardens. Give *Ginkgo biloba* a sunny position and fertile, freely draining soil.

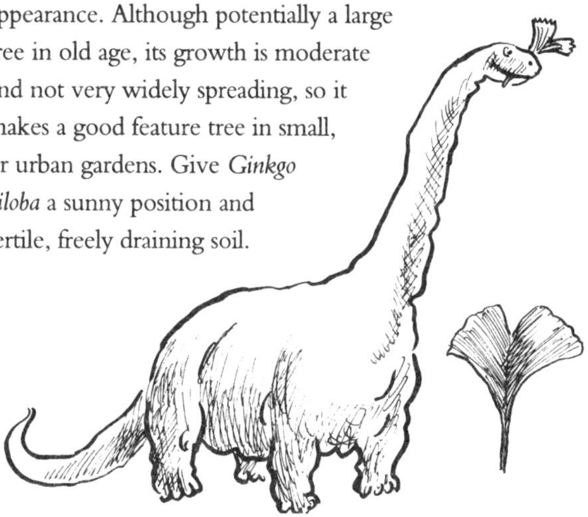

The field maple

The genus *Acer* has around 150 different species, ranging from short shrubs to tall, stately trees. Of the species that are planted in gardens, the most familiar are the highly ornamental Japanese kinds; but there is also a native English maple, *Acer campestre*, popularly known as the field maple. Its natural habitat is open woods, hedgerows and coppices, especially in southern Britain.

The field maple makes a very pretty garden tree: it is slow growing and of small-to-medium stature, and it is versatile, too, as it can be trimmed to a neat outline in a formal garden, perhaps as a lawn specimen; it also makes an excellent hedging plant, which looks especially decorative in mixed country hedges in the company of hawthorn, guelder rose and honeysuckle.

December

Gardening books and magazines always show gardens in winter crisply iced with hoary frost, and very tempting they look, too. Many of us though (and certainly those of us in the south and west) seldom experience these Christmas card-like conditions, and even then only fleetingly and usually at sunrise: for us, midwinter is often mild, and let's face it, soggy; the lawn may even still be growing, albeit ever so slowly. Our compensation is that we can continue to put new plants, hedges

and trees in the ground. If it is cold, though, spare a thought for the garden birds, and ensure that they have regular supplies of food and water.

ORNAMENTAL GARDEN

Trees & Shrubs

Continue planting any new deciduous trees and shrubs. In very mild areas, container-grown evergreens can still be planted out. Elsewhere, leave them until spring, as cold weather causes them too much stress before their roots are established.

If snow falls, use a broom to sweep it off evergreen trees and shrubs that might be damaged by its weight. Check that ties around columnar yews, junipers and other conifers are strong and secure.

Sowing

Sow ripened seeds of hawthorn, cotoneaster, mountain ash, and pyracantha. Squash the berries to extract the seeds, which should be cleaned of all the pulp before sowing. Sow them in small pots filled with gritty compost, and cover with a layer of grit. Gently water, and stand pots outdoors, or in a well-ventilated cold-frame.

Lawns

Give the lawn what may be its last mowing for the season, depending on weather. Send mowing machinery for cleaning and servicing now, rather than when you need it again in spring.

During mild and dry weather, improve soil aeration and drainage on the lawn by removing plugs of soil with a hollow-tined aerator. Push the aerator into the ground at roughly 6-inch (15cm) intervals. Refill the holes with a mixture of two parts coarse sand and one part potting compost.

Pruning

Clematis

Hard-prune late-flowering clematis, such as *C. viticella, texensis* and *tangutica* species, and their hybrids. (The cultivars 'Gipsy Queen', 'Hagley Hybrid', 'Jackmanii', 'Perle d'Azur', 'Star of India', and 'Ville de Lyon' fall into this category.) Cut back to near ground level, above a strong pair of buds on each stem, and dispose of all the old growth above. Don't prune spring-flowering clematis, however, or you'll lose next year's flowers.

Winter Protection

Hellebore buds

If you want to ensure that you have some perfect Christmas rose (*Helleborus niger*) blooms to cut for indoors, use cloches over the plants to protect the emerging flowerbuds.

Alpines

To prevent outdoor alpines from rotting in winter wet, cover with a firmly propped-up pane of glass that allows free passage of air. Woolly or grey-

❋ *Quick Tips* ❋

The foot of an old stocking tied to the inlet of a water-butt will collect any grit from the roof. *Elizabeth Oakland*

To protect an outside water tap from freezing, wrap a wet towel around it. Ice formed on the towel insulates the tap. *R A Selway*

leaved varieties are often susceptible. Remove any dead and decaying leaves from around plants and top up the surface dressing of grit.

Routine Care & Maintenance

Continue removing and composting fallen leaves, but burn any from blackspot-infested roses. Turn the compost heap and ensure it has a closely fitting lid to help maintain heat.

Tools

This is a good time to clean and sharpen garden tools, and also to drop hints about which ones are due for replacement. Gardeners are easy to buy presents for, but if you're very particular about the brands of tool you use, ensure that you let everyone know (in the most subtle way, of course).

Paths

Use a knife to clear weeds that have self-sown in the joints of paving and on path edges.

Timber

Restore or replace trelliswork and other timber structures now, while plants are dormant.

Mulching
Try to complete mulching of flowerbeds; it is a more difficult job to do when spring bulbs and flowers are pushing through.

Birds & Fish

Hang feeders for birds, and ensure they are refilled regularly. Once the birds are accustomed to your hospitality, they will rely on you for food. Not all birds are nut and seed feeders; some prefer fruit or fatty scraps so, if possible, provide a varied buffet.

Ensure that fishponds do not completely freeze over. Float a rubber ball on the pond's surface to keep one area ice-free, or use a saucepan of hot water to melt a hole as needed.

KITCHEN GARDEN

Fruit

Trees
Prune apple and pear trees (but not plums and cherries, which are susceptible to disease when pruned in winter). Pruning at this time of year encourages strong new growth. Cut this year's whippy stems back to leave about five buds on each, and take out crossing or damaged branches. Apply some slow-release general fertiliser to the ground around the root area.

Vines
Also prune grape-vines now, while they are dormant. If left until late winter the sap will be rising and will bleed copiously from every cut. Prune back this year's lateral stems to leave one strong bud on each. Renew ties on the framework.

Rhubarb
This is a good time to plant new rhubarb, and to divide large clumps.

Digging

Try to finish digging jobs before the new year, when weather tends to be colder and the soil less easily worked.

INDOORS & UNDER GLASS

Early sweet-peas
Pinch out tips of sweet-peas sown last month to create bushier growth.

Alpine seeds
Sow seeds of alpine plants that require cold winter temperatures in order to germinate. Sow into shallow pots or trays filled with sharply draining gritty compost, and place outdoors in a cold-frame.

Quick Tip

Stop the legs of ladders sinking into soft earth or turf by fitting empty tins over the legs. *Leslie Baverstock*

Poinsettia
Keep Christmas poinsettias healthy by placing them in an evenly warm room, away from draughts or radiators. Mist-spray the leaves with water regularly to prevent them turning yellow or shrivelled (poinsettias need moister air than most centrally heated rooms can offer). Standing the plants on trays of wet gravel also helps.

Potted plants
Check greenhouse plants regularly. Remove dead or decaying leaves, and dispose of aphids hiding in soft growth at the tips. Water plants sparingly as required, preferably in the morning so there is the rest of the day for moisture to evaporate. Provide emerging winter bulbs and flowering pot-plants with a weak liquid feed.

Unusual seeds
Sow something unusual in the new year. The regularly revised directory, *The Seed Search* by Karen

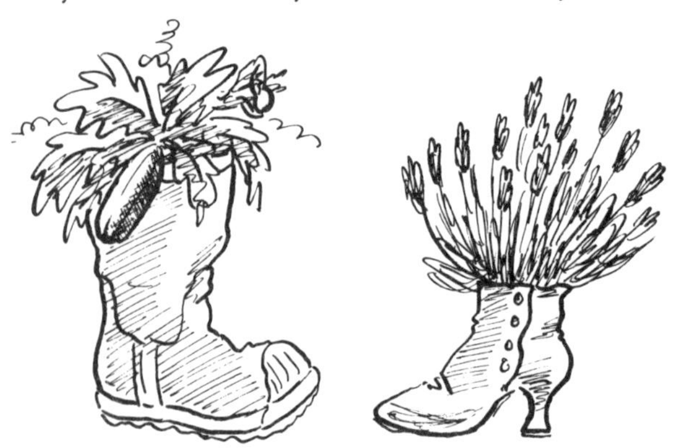

Quick Tip

Save your old boots for planting up as unusual containers for bedding plants. *E M Warner*

Platt, lists seeds of over 43,000 different plants, including 6,000 vegetables, and where you can buy them. It is available at £13.74 (including postage), from Karen Platt (35 Longfield Road, Crookes, Sheffield, S10 1QW. Tel/fax 0114 268 1700).

Ventilation
Check that any crops under glass (including cold frames) have adequate daytime ventilation.

Root-cuttings
Take root-cuttings of perennial *Gypsophila*, *Crambe*, *Eryngium*, *Acanthus*, *Catananche*, *Echinops*, *Gaillardia*, Japanese anemones, oriental poppies, *Phlox*, *Trollius* and *Romneya*. Take 2–4 inch (5–10cm) long pieces of healthy root cut from near the crown. Dust with fungicide and plunge into pots or trays of seed compost. Cover the surface with grit, and keep in a cold-frame or cold greenhouse. They don't need extra heat, but keep an eye on progress and pot on when new shoots emerge in spring.

QUESTIONS & ANSWERS

When is the best time to prune a mixed hedgerow hedge, which forms the boundary between myself and my neighbour? It includes a whole mix of things – hawthorn, ivy, some beech, privet, and goodness knows what else.

R Foreman, Wimborne

Any time during autumn and winter should be fine, but don't leave it until the spring, when wild birds will be choosing and building their nesting sites.

When I cut open an avocado pear recently, I was astonished to find the stone inside had slightly split, and started sprouting a tiny shoot. I potted it up, and it has since grown into a leafy plant. Can I expect my own home-grown supply of avocados in the future?

Katy J Graham, Oxford

Avocado plants are quite fun to grow from the stones, although they don't always germinate. (Maybe because they are chilled in transportation, or too unripe when picked?) You were lucky to have a head start but, to be honest, they are not the most interesting of house or conservatory plants. Unfortunately, they don't set flowers or fruits in this country, so you – and I – shall have to continue depending on the shops for our supplies of the fleshy fruits.

Every year in autumn I plant a few handfuls of crocuses and other bulbs, but they always seem to be attacked (by rodents, I think). How can I protect my bulbs and get the spring display I have always hoped for?

J Reynolds, Richmond

Mice and squirrels are sure to be the culprits but there is a way of spoiling their depredations. Cover the bulb-planted area with fine-mesh wire which will prevent them digging out the bulbs. You can leave it there, because the leaves and shoots will grow through the mesh and flower as usual. This is another instance where a pet cat can also be a useful deterrent.

Looking Good in December ...

Algerian iris

From a mound of strappy evergreen leaves, the flowers of the Algerian iris, *Iris unguicularis*, emerge in the dead of winter. Unlike their bold, showy cousins – the bearded irises that flower from late spring to midsummer – this winter bloomer is shy and discreet, bearing its soft lavender flowers on short stems, often half-hidden among the foliage.

One of its great assets is its attractiveness as a cut flower. Cut the stems at the fat-bud stage, just before the flowers have opened, and bring them indoors; as they begin to open, they will fill the room with a sweet scent. Algerian iris is perfect for poor, well-drained soil at the foot of a south-facing wall, where the rhizomes can bake in summer. Plant new ones in groups, 1 inch (2.5cm) deep, in September.

Variegated holly

'Then Heigh-ho! the holly! This life is most jolly!' sings Amiens in Shakespeare's *As You Like It*. And holly is certainly most jolly in its variegated forms at this time of year. One of the best is *Ilex* x *altaclerensis* 'Lawsoniana' – bold and bright with scarlet berries and very dark-green, almost spineless leaves splashed with exotic lemon-and-lime markings. 'Madame Briot' has a butter-coloured ribbon around the edge of its spiny leaves; purple stems and crimson-washed new foliage are a bonus.

Hollies are easy to grow in most soils, but female trees need a male holly nearby for pollination if they are to produce berries (garden centres will advise). Prune off plain dark-green or yellow shoots that may arise, to preserve the plant's variegated foliage (it will otherwise revert to the plain-coloured variety).

GARDENING FOR WILDLIFE

A garden without birds, butterflies, bees and abundant varieties of insects and small mammals would be a sterile place, however beautiful its flowers. As the destruction of woods, meadows, hedgerows and wetlands continues to diminish our native wildlife's natural habitats, our help is acutely needed by the specialised range of creatures that make up the web of life itself. Gardeners can do their bit to help and – fortunately – it's not difficult.

Birds

Just by growing a broad range of plants you can attract birds to your garden. Some, such as finches, are seed-eaters, while others – tits, wrens and robins – usefully eat caterpillars, aphids and other insects. Birds encouraged to dine in your garden in winter on nuts, seeds, fat and kitchen scraps, will repay you in warmer seasons by eating pests, singing merry tunes, and keeping you company.

Provide nest-boxes with tiny entrance holes for tits and nuthatches, and open-fronted ones for robins, positioned out of reach of predators (including cats). Grow berrying hedges such as hawthorn, pyracantha, Rugosa roses, guelder rose and ivy – even a mixture of these – to provide food, security and nesting opportunities.

It is of course true that bullfinches will ravage plum blossom, blackbirds peck the best ripening fruits, and pigeons and pheasants can wreak havoc in the vegetable garden, but there are friendly ways of keeping them off specific plants. Protect crops with fleece or Enviromesh fabrics (sold by the metre in garden centres), or split-bamboo cages (Andrew Crace, Hertfordshire, tel. 01279 842685). Grow small tree and bush fruits in fruit-cages, and protect the best trusses of fruit on larger trees with bags made of muslin or Enviromesh.

Butterflies & Bees

Butterflies love nectar-rich flowers – *Centaurea*, sedums, scabious, thymes, hyssop, Michaelmas daisies, sweet rocket, verbenas and, of course, the 'butterfly bush' (buddleia) – and their caterpillars thrive in meadow grasses, buckthorn, lady's smock, trefoils, thistles, and nettles. Moths enjoy fragrant evening flowers, such as night-scented stock and evening primrose. Bees, too, go for nectar-rich flowers and for pollen. Conservationists will urge you to grow native flowers – no bad thing – but many garden hybrids and introduced species are just as valuable: rosemary, lavender, salvias, pelargoniums, pieris, heathers, echinops and heleniums, to name a few.

A new approach

Perhaps the most valuable and lasting way of bringing back a garden's wildlife is to go organic or, at least, adopt a no-spray policy. Compost garden waste and green kitchen scraps, and apply manure mulches and well-rotted compost or leaf-mould to enrich soil with the correct balance of bacteria, air and soil organisms. A previously sprayed garden will take two or three years to recover its natural eco-system. In the meantime, you can create a diverse range of habitats by planting various shrubs, perennials and annual flowers, and the odd tree for shade and shelter. Good trees for small gardens include field maple, crab apple, smaller varieties of cherry, and the willow-leaved pear, *Pyrus salicifolia* 'Pendula'.

In winter, keep leaf-mounds or wood-piles for hibernating hedgehogs; and leave some seeds in flowerheads for birds to supplement their diet. Ponds are invaluable habitats for frogs and toads (both effective slug-hunters), for dragonflies, newts, water snails, the insects sought by birds and, of course, for water and marshland plants.

Plant your Name

Some people have almost unlimited choice when it comes to planting their name: Rose, Hebe, Iris, Nigella, Daphne, and Rosemary have entire genera at their disposal. If my name were Daisy, I might be tempted to collect some of the plants belonging to the vast daisy family (Asteraceae, formerly listed as Compositae), which consists of plants and flowers as diverse as sunflowers, artichokes, dahlias, gerberas, and autumn's Michaelmas daisies.

Most of us, however, are not named after plants; but there are cultivars named after us, or at any rate someone who shares our name. In researching this section I came across two cultivars named Kathryn, and many names belonging to family and friends.

The majority of cultivar names are female, presumably because plants have so often been named by nurserymen or keen gardeners after their wives and daughters. Joy, Laura, Stella and Wendy crop up time and again; more surprisingly, there are also many Carmens and Merlins. Diana, Elizabeth and Victoria appear frequently, no doubt because of their associations with royalty; just as popular, however, is Dawn, who has almost a gardenful of plants to her name. Either Dawn is someone very special, or plant breeders have frequently found their inspiration in the sunrise.

FINDING YOUR PLANT

The easiest way to find a stockist of your namesake plant is to consult *The Plant Finder*, a hefty directory (published by Dorling Kindersley, £12.99; CD Rom, £25) that lists plants by genera and gives the names of nurseries that sell them (often by mail order). *The Seed Search*, by Karen Platt (*see* page 137), lists the relatively few cultivars (and vegetables) that are available as seed, and their stockists.

HOW TO USE THIS LIST

Cultivars are listed alphabetically in bold (with the inverted commas in which they usually appear omitted). Family and genus names (such as Lily and Daphne) are not included unless they also happen to be the name of a cultivar. To save space, slightly unusual name spellings are listed under the more conventional spelling, except in cases where the initial letter differs (Gemma and Jemma, for example) or where there are so many cultivars for each spelling that two entries are warranted. Alternative spellings appear in brackets after the relevant genus or species, so:

Alison *Pelargonium, Rosa, Viola, Dianthus alpinus* ('Alyson')

From this it will be understood that *Pelargonium, Rosa and Viola* have cultivars bearing the name Alison; *Dianthus alpinus* has one called Alyson. Some cultivars are Latinised (as in Douglasii); these will be found under the main entry (Douglas in this case). Sometimes a name forms only part of that of a cultivar, as in 'Fair Bianca'; these, too, are given in brackets after the relevant plant genus or species.

Abigail *Rosa, Viola*
Adam *Ficus carica* (fig), *Hedera helix, Monarda, Rosa*
Adele *Pelargonium*
Adrian *Primula auricula, Salvia* x *superba*
Agatha *Rosa*
Agnes *Rosa*
Ailsa *Pelargonium*
Alan *Hemerocallis*
Alanah *Clematis, Geranium* x *lidavicum*
Alastair *Lathyrus odoratus*
Albert *Erica arborea* ('Albert's Gold')
Albertina *Fuchsia*
Albertine *Rosa*
Alcea *Viola*
Alena *Rhododendron*
Alethea *Fuchsia*
Alex *Pelargonium*
Alexander *Clematis, Malus domestica* (apple), *Phlox paniculata, Rhododendron* (azalea), *Rosa*
Alexandra *Bougainvillea, Fragaria vesca* (strawberry)
Alexia *Viola*
Alfie *Fuchsia*
Alfred *Rhododendron*
Algernon *Pelargonium*
Alice *Dianthus, Gladiolus, Rhododendron* (azalea)
Alicia *Calluna vulgaris, Primula auricula*
Alison *Pelargonium, Rosa, Viola, Dianthus alpinus* ('Alyson')
Alma *Ficus carica* (fig), leek, *Pelargonium, Ribes uva-matis, Viola*
Alwyn *Viola*
Amanda *Rosa, Sempervivum, Streptocarpus*
Amber *Kniphofia*
Amelia *Leucanthemum* x *superbum, Rosa, Viola*
Amy *Calluna vulgaris, Begonia*
Anastasia Iris (tall-bearded)
Andrea *Lophomyrtus* x *ralphii, Rhododendron*
Andrew *Dianthus, Fuchsia*
Angela *Fuchsia, Viola*
Angelique *Ficus carica* (fig), *Tulipa*
Angelina *Rosa*
Angeline *Fuchsia*
Angelo *Dianthus*
Anita *Clematis, Fuchsia, Rhododendron, Viola*
Anja *Aster* ('Anja's Choice'), *Phlox* x *arendsii*
Ann *Magnolia, Rosa, Viola*
Anna *Calluna vulgaris, Clematis, Pelargonium, Rubus arcticus, Viola*
Annabel *Calluna vulgaris, Clematis*, dwarf French bean, *Fuchsia, Helianthemum, Rosa* ('Annabell')
Annabella *Rhododendron* (azalea)
Annabelle *Dianthus, Hydrangea arborescens, Lathyrus odoratus, Viola*

Anna-Louise *Clematis*
Anna Marie *Hyacinthus orientalis*
Anne *Primula allionii, Streptocarpus, Verbena* ('Silver Anne')
Anneke *Aster novi-belgii, Calluna vulgaris, Rhododendron* (azalea)
Anneliese *Viola*
Annette *Dianthus, Potentilla fruticosa, Calluna vulgaris* ('Anette')
Anne Marie *Calluna vulgaris* ('Annemarie'), *Hedera hibernca*
Anny *Rhododendron* (azalea)
Anya Potato
Anthea *Achillea, Viola*
Anthony *Matthiola incana*
Anuschka *Rhododendron*
Arabella *Calluna vulgaris, Clematis, Fuchsia, Viola*
Ariadne *Calluna vulgaris*
Ariane *Phlox stolonifera, Primula obconica*
Arlene *Dianthus*
Arnold *Juniperus communis, Liriodendron tulipifera*
Arthur *Dianthus*
Ashley *Dianthus*
Astrid *Rhododendron, Viola*
Audrey *Aster novi-belgii, Pelargonium, Syringa*
Augusta *Pelargonium, Rubus idaeus* (raspberry),
Aurelia *Viola*
Aurora *Amaranthus tricolor, Clarkia amoena, Fuchsia* ('Pink Aurora'), *Rhododendron* (azalea), *Tagetes patula, Viburnum carlesii, Viola*
Austin *Primula auricula*
Avril *Pelargonium, Viola*

Babette *Fuchsia*
Barbara *Fuchsia, Viola*
Barbara Ann *Begonia*
Beatrice *Hebe,* lettuce, *Primula auricula, Viola*
Beatrix *Pelargonium*
Becky *Fuchsia*
Belinda *Hippeastrum*
Bella *Astilbe* x *arendsii, Campanula medium,* cucumber, *Dianthus, Viola*
Ben *Camellia sasanqua, Rhododendron* ('Little Ben')
Benjamin *Pinus mugo, Rhododendron* ('Benjamen')
Bernadette *Fuchsia*
Bernice *Campanula traclum*
Beryl *Fuchsia* ('Beryl's Choice'), *Streptocarpus*
Bess *Begonia*
Beth *Pyrus communis* (pear)
Betsy *Centranthus ruber*
Bettina *Rosa, Saxifraga, Viola*
Betty *Hosta, Phlox subulata, Rhododendron* (azalea), *Viola*
Beverley *Fuchsia*

Bianca *Fuchsia, Rosa* ('Fair Bianca'), *Viola*
Bobby *Fuchsia* ('Bobby boy'), *Dianthus*
Bonny *Fuchsia*
Boris *Geum* ('Borisii')
Branwen *Streptocarpus*
Brenda *Fuchsia, Pelargonium, Tanacetum coccineum*
Bridget *Lathyrus odoratus*
Brien *Juniperus communis*
Bronwen *Viola*
Bruce *Delphinium*
Bryony *Viola*
Bunty *Primula auricula*

Caesar *Matthiola*
Camilla *Dianthus, Pelargonium*
Candida *Galanthus* x *hartlandii, Nymphaea candida, Primula auricula, Viola*
Candy *Pelargonium*
Caprice *Petunia*
Carina *Tagetes tenuifolia, Viola*
Carl *Sedum*
Carla Chicory
Carlotta *Dianthus, Lathyrus odoratus*
Carmel *Smithiantha*
Carmen *Calluna vulgaris*, cucumber, *Dianthus, Fuchsia, Paeonia lactiflora, Primula, Rhododendron, Rosa, Saxifraga, Sempervivum, Tagetes patula*
Carmen Maria *Fuchsia*
Carol *Pelargonium* ('Carole'), *Primula auricula* ('Carole'), *Rosa, Santolina chamaecyparissus* ('Pretty Carol'), *Streptocarpus*
Carola *Viola*
Caroline *Clematis, Fuchsia, Nerine, Viola*
Carolyn *Calluna vulgaris*
Carrie *Hosta*
Casper *Dianthus*
Cassandra *Viola*
Cassius *Delphinium*
Catherine *Erica carnea, Fuchsia* ('Catherina'), *Lathyrus odoratus, Nerine, Primula auricula*
Catrin *Streptocarpus*
Catriona *Osteospermum*
Cecile *Fuchsia, Rhododendron* (azalea)
Cecily *Aster novi-belgii*
Cedric *Salvia officinalis,*
Celeste *Rosa*
Celina *Rosa*
Ceri *Fuchsia*
Chantal *Viola*
Charity *Dianthus, Erigeron, Mahonia, Pelargonium, Viola*
Charles *Dianthus, Fuchsia* ('Big Charles'), *Tulipa*
Charlotte *Echinops ritro, Malus domestica* (apple), rhubarb, chard, potato *Rosa, Viola*
Charmaine *Phlox paniculata*
Charmian *Rosa*

Cherie *Pelargonium*
Cheryl *Dianthus, Fuchsia*
Chloe *Primula auricula, Viola*
Chris *Fuchsia*
Chrissie *Pelargonium*
Christabel *Gladiolus, Viola* ('Christobel')
Christina *Aster novi-belgii, Calluna vulgaris,* cauliflower, *Viola*
Christine *Primula* x *pubescens, Saxifraga*
Christopher *Dianthus, Gazania, Rosa,*
Cindy *Erica cinerea, Kohl-rabi, Pelargonium, Primula auricula, Sempervivum, Viola*
Circe *Delphinium, Fuchsia*
Clara *Begonia, Dianthus*
Clarabel *Nerine*
Clare *Delphinium* ('Claire'), *Dianthus, Narcissus, Nerium oleander, Pleione formosana, Primula auricula, Viola* ('Claire')
Clarence *Hosta, Parahebe lyallii*
Clarissa *Nerine, Pelargonium, Rhododendron* (azalea), *Rosa*
Claudette Brussels sprout
Claudia *Hosta, Paeonia*
Clementina *Viola*
Clementine Tomato
Cleo *Viola*
Cleopatra *Begonia, Matthiola incana, Pelargonium, Rosa*
Clodagh *Viola*
Colette *Calluna vulgaris, Pelargonium, Viola*
Colleen *Viola*
Connie *Fuchsia, Primula auricula, Viola*
Constance *Clematis alpina, Dianthus, Fuchsia, Aster ericoides*
Cordelia *Galanthus, Viola*
Corinne *Lathyrus odoratus*
Cressida *Delphinium, Rosa, Viola*
Cymbeline *Rosa*
Cynthia Lettuce, *Rhododendron, Streptocarpus, Tulipa clusiana*

Daisy Dwarf French bean
Dana *Saxifraga*
Danae *Rosa*
Dandy *Aster novi-belgii, Calabrese,* dwarf bean, *Rhododendron*
Daniela *Aster novi-belgii*
Daphne *Dianthus, Lathyrus odoratus,* Savoy cabbage
Darius *Nerine*
David *Bergenia, Dianthus, Fuchsia, Helianthemum, Nymphaea, Phlox paniculata, Viola* ('Little David')
Davina *Pelargonium, Viola*
Dawn *Clematis, Dianthus, Erica* x *watsonii, Fuchsia, Helleborus orientalis, Hosta, Lathyrus odoratus, Narcissus, Pelargonium,*

Rhodohypoxis, Saxifraga, Viburnum x *bodnantense, Viola*
Deanna *Viola*
Debbie *Camellia japonica, Fuchsia* ('Debby' and 'Miss Debbie'), *Hebe*
Dee *Erica tetralix*
Delia *Hosta, Saxifraga, Viola*
Delilah *Fuchsia*
Delphine *Viola*
Denis *Dianthus*
Denise *Paeonia lactiflora*
Denisa *Saxifraga*
Desdemona *Galanthus, Syringa, Viola*
Desiree *Calluna vulgaris*, potato, runner bean
Desmond *Dianthus*
Diana *Aster novi-belgii, Begonia, Calluna vulgaris*, cucumber, *Fuchsia, Hebe, Hibiscus, Lathyrus odoratus*, lettuce, *Papaver orientale, Streptocarpus, Tulipa, Viburnum carlesii*
Diane *Begonia* ('Sweet Dianne'), *Dianthus, Hamamelis, Hebe* ('Dianne'), *Pelargonium, Penstemon, Primula auricula, Rhododendron*
Dido *Rhododendron*
Dilys *Geranium*
Dolly *Aster novi-belgii*, endive, lettuce
Dimity *Erigeron, Viola*
Dominic *Hemerocallis*
Donna *Tulipa* ('Donna Bella')
Dora *Dianthus*
Doreen *Rosa*
Doris *Dianthus*
Dorothea *Rhododendron*
Dorothy *Aquilegia, Crocus chrysanthus, Fuchsia, Gazania, Hosta, Primula*
Douglas *Rhodohypoxis, Phlox* ('Douglasii'), *Sedum* ('Douglasii')
Dulcie *Rhodohypoxis baurii*
Duncan Cabbage

Eddie *Cornus* ('Eddie's White Wonder')
Edith *Clematis, Fuchsia, Hypericum olympicum, Saxifraga*
Edna *Dianthus*
Eileen *Dianthus, Rhododendron*
Eilidh *Dianthus*
Elaine *Begonia, Calluna vulgaris, Helianthemum*
Eleanor *Gentiana*
Elfrida *Fuchsia*
Elina *Rosa*
Elinor *Syringa*
Elisha *Viola*
Elizabeth *Aster novi-belgii, Clematis montana, Diascia, Erodium, Gentiana, Hosta* ('Elisabeth') *Lathyrus odoratus, Magnolia, Passiflora, Potentilla fruitcosa, Rhododendron* (azalea), *Sempervivum, Viola*

Elizabeth Jane *Leptospermum scoparium*
Ella *Lathyrus odoratus*
Ellen *Calluna vulgaris, Hebe, Hosta, Rosa*
Ellie *Astilbe* x *arendsii*
Elliott *Vaccinium*
Elsa *Fuchsia*
Elsie *Primula auricula, Streptocarpus* ('Elsi')
Elspeth *Nerine, Rhododendron*
Elvira *Gladiolus*
Elvis *Sempervivum*
Emanuel *Rosa*
Emily *Fragaria* x *ananassa* (strawberry), *Nerium oleander* ('Emilie'), *Potentilla* ('Emilie'), *Rosa*
Emma *Diascia, Viola*
Emma Louise *Pelargonium*
Eric *Bergenia* ('Eric's Best'), *Helleborus orientalis* ('Eric's Best')
Erica *Aster novi-belgii, Astilbe* x *arendsii, Veronica spicata* ('Erika')
Esther *Dahlia, Pulmonaria*
Ethel *Rhododendron, Rosa*
Eva *Aster novi-belgii, Callistephus, Hedera helix, Phlox douglasii*
Eva-Kate *Rhodohypoxis*
Eveline *Dahlia*
Evelyn *Pelargonium, Penstemon, Rosa*

Fabia *Rhododendron*
Faith *Aster novi-belgii, Mahonia*
Fanny *Rhododendron*
Fatima *Camellia japonica, Lathyrus odoratus*
Felicia *Rosa*
Felicity *Erigeron, Hemerocallis, Viola*
Felix *Viola*
Fenella *Delphinium*
Fifi *Rosa*
Fiona *Dianthus, Fuchsia, Lathyrus odoratus, Pulmonaria, Rosa, Streptocarpus, Viola*
Flavia *Fuchsia*
Fleur *Dianthus*
Flora *Rosa*
Florence *Centaurea cyanus*, dwarf bean, strawberry, *Viola*
Frances *Erica cinerea, Lobelia, Viola*
Francesca *Rosa, Viola*
Francis *Hedera helix*
Frankie *Clematis*
Freda *Clematis montana*
Freddie *Gazania, Stromanthe* ('Freddy')
Freya *Rhododendron* (azalea)

Gabriel *Pelargonium*
Gabrielle *Clematis, Rhododendron* ('Gabriele', azalea)
Gail *Larix* x *marschlinsii*
Galahad *Sempervivum*

Gemma *Delphinium, Pelargonium, Viola*
Georgana *Fuchsia*
George *Berberis* ('Georgei')
Georgette *Rhododendron, Sempervivum*
Georgia *Geranium* ('Georgia Blue'), *Pelargonium, Veronica peduncularis* ('Georgia Blue')
Georgina *Nemesia, Viola*
Geraldine *Fuchsia, Pelargonium, Viola*
Gilda *Fuchsia*
Gillian *Gladiolus, Parahebe*
Gina *Viola*
Ginger *Rhododendron* (azalea), *Salvia officinalis*
Giselle *Viola*
Gladys *Saxifraga*
Gloria *Astilbe* x *arendsii, Celosia plumosa, Chrysanthemum segetum, Cosmos bipinnatus, Crocosmia* x *crocosmiiflora, Rhododendron, Saxifraga burseriana, Streptocarpus*
Godiva *Saxifraga*
Goldie *Solenostemon*
Grace *Clarkia amoena, Cotinus, Fuchsia, Viola*
Gracie *Fuchsia* ('Our Gracie')
Greta *Fuchsia, Rhododendron* (azalea)
Griselda *Viola*
Gwen *Erica* x*watsonii, Primula auricula*
Gwenda *Rhododendron* (azalea)
Gwendoline *Lathyrus odoratus*

Hamilton *Tulipa, Vaccinium*
Hannah *Fuchsia* ('Hanna'), *Pelargonium*
Harriett *Fuchsia*
Hazel *Fuchsia, Hosta, Primula auricula*
Hebe *Hebe, Viola*
Hecktor *Verbena*
Heidi *Aquilegia vulgaris, Dianthus, Hebe, Pelargonium, Streptocarpus*
Helen *Aster novi-belgii, Dianthus, Erodium, Primula auricula, Rhodohypoxis, Rubus fruticosus, Streptocarpus, Viola*
Helena *Hedera hibernica, Pelargonium, Primula auricula, Viola*
Henry *Clematis* ('Henryi'), *Gentiana, Itea virginica* ('Henry's Garnet')
Herbert *Vaccinium*
Hermione *Pelargonium*
Hester *Calluna vulgaris, Sempervivum*
Hetty *Calluna vulgaris*
Hilda *Phlox* x *arendsii*
Hippolyte *Rosa*
Holly *Lewisia, Phlox subulata, Solenostemon*
Hope *Camellia* x *williamsii, Dianthus, Pelargonium*

Horatio *Fuchsia*
Hugh *Rosa* ('Master Hugh')
Hyacinth *Astilbe* x *arendsii*

Ian *Dianthus*
Iantha *Viola*
Igor *Papaver somniferum*
Iolanthe *Fuchsia, Magnolia*
Irene *Aster novi-belgii, Nymphaea, Pelargonium*
Irina *Viola*
Iris *Dahlia, Phlox paniculata*
Isabelina *Digitalis*
Isabel *Erica carnea, Nerium oleander* ('Isabelle'), *Pelargonium, Viola* ('Isobel')
Isabella *Rosa, Syringa*
Isla *Viola*
Ivan *Geranium*
Ivana *Saxifraga*
Ivonne *Chamaecyparis lawsoniana*

Jackie *Pelargonium, Verbascum*
Jacqueline *Fuchsia, Schefflera*
Jade Broad bean, corn-salad, dwarf bean, *Fuchsia* ('Pink Jade')
James *Pelargonium* ('Baby James'), *Biola*
Jan *Calluna vulgaris*
Jane *Magnolia, Sempevivum*
Janet *Erica cinerea, Hosta, Nerine, Primula auricula, Primula marginata, Viola*
Janette *Geranium*
Janie *Fuchsia*
Janine *Viola*
Jason *Saxifraga*
Jasper *Hebe, Hedera helix, Sempervivum*
Jean *Aster novi-belgii, Erica carnea, Fuchsia* ('Jeane')
Jeanette *Rhododendron* (azalea)
Jemma *Rosa, Viola*
Jennifer *Pelargonium, Schizostylis, Streptocarpus*
Jenny *Aster novi-belgii, Calluna vulgaris, Narcissus, Primula allionii, Primula auricula, Viola*
Jess *Fuchsia*
Jessica *Rosa* ('Pretty Jessica'), *Viola*
Jill *Nerine*
Jilly *Lathyrus odoratus*
Jimmy *Tulipa*
Jo Dwarf bean
Joan *Nerine*
Joanna *Erythronium, Hebe, Streptocarpus, Viola*
Johanna *Primula, Rhododendron* (azalea), *Tulipa*
Joanne *Dianthus, Papaver orientale, Primula auricula, Rosa*
Jocelyn *Rosa*
Jock *Dianthus* ('Little Jock')
Joel *Fuchsia, Primula auricula*

Joella *Viola*
Johnny *Fuchsia, Viola* ('Little Johnny')
Josefine *Calluna vulgaris*
Josie *Viola*
Joy *Aubrieta, Dianthus, Geranium, Parahebe, Pelargonium, Penstemon, Primula auricula, Petunia, Saxifraga*
Joyce *Primula auricula*
Judith *Aster novi-belgii, Nerine*
Judy *Dianthus, Hebe, Magnolia*
Julia *Aster novi-belgii, Calluna vulgaris, Fuchsia, Pelargonium, Primula allionii, P. auricula, Rubus idaeus* (raspberry), *Viola*
Julian *Dianthus, Viola*
Juliana *Lathyrus odoratus*
Juliane *Papaver orientale*
Julie *Larix* x *marschlinsii, Streptocarpus*
Juliet *Rosa, Saxifraga, Tagetes patula* ('Juliette'), *Viola* ('Juliette')
June *Hemerocallis*

Karen *Fuchsia, Phlox* ('Miss Karen'), *Streptocarpus*
Karin *Begonia, Rhododendron*
Kate *Diascia, Geranium, Viola*
Katerina *Viola*
Katherine *Clematis, Malus*
Kathleen *Rhododendron* (azalea), *Rosa, Saxifraga*
Kathryn *Lophomyrtus* x *ralphii, Pelargonium*
Kathy Lettuce, *Primula auricula, Viola*
Kathy Louise *Fuchsia*
Katie *Camellia japonica, Hemerocallis, Pittosporum tenuifolium, Rosa*
Katinka *Rhododendron* (azalea), *Viola*
Katisha *Rhododendron* (azalea)
Katrina *Fuchsia*
Katy *Malus domestica* (apple)
Kelly *Castanea dentata*
Kelvin Lettuce
Kerrie *Viola*
Kerry Ann *Fuchsia*
Kerstin *Calluna vulgaris*
Kim *Primula auricula, Rosa, Streptocarpus, Syringa* ('Miss Kim')
Kimberley *Lithops lesliei*
Kip *Sempervivum*
Kirsten *Potentilla nepalensis*
Kirsty *Viola*
Kitty *Camellia japonica, Narcissus* ('Miss Kitty')
Kristin *Rosa*
Kristina *Aster novi-belgii*
Kristy *Pelargonium*
Kylie *Aster*

Lana *Begonia*
Lancelot *Begonia*, leek
Larissa *Fuchsia*

Laura *Clematis, Dianthus,* dwarf French bean, *Fragaria* x *ananassa* (strawberry), *Fuchsia, Lathyrus odoratus,* leek, *Magnolia, Pelargonium, Phlox paniculata, Streptocarpus, Viola*
Laurie *Fuchsia*
Laurin *Tanacetum coccineum*
Lavinia *Galanthus, Rosa, Viola*
Lawrence *Viola*
Leander *Rosa, Viola*
Leda *Rosa, Viola*
Lena *Cytisus, Fuchsia*
Leni *Rhododendron*
Lenny *Hibiscus, Rhododendron* ('Leny'),
Leo *Doronicum* ('Little Leo'), *Helleborus orientalis, Pelargonium, Rhododendron* (and azalea), *Rubus idaeus* (raspberry)
Leonora *Fuchsia, Tradescantia* x *andersoniana*
Leonore *Gladiolus, Saxifraga*
Lesley *Fuchsia*
Letitia *Pelargonium, Verbascum, Viola*
Lianne *Viola*
Lilian *Gaultheria mucronata,* lettuce, *Pelargonium*
Liliana *Rosa, Viola*
Lillibet *Fuchsia*
Linda *Catharanthus roseus* ('Little Linda'), *Hemerocallis, Lavatera, Malus domestica* (apple), *Pelargonium, Rhododendron, Rubus arcticus*
Lindsey *Pelargonium*
Lindy *Fuchsia*
Lisa *Eustoma, Ficus c arica* (fig), *Fuchsia, Pelargonium, Primula auricula, Streptocarpus*
Livia *Viola*
Liz *Fuchsia*
Lizbeth *Lathyrus odoratus*
Lizzie *Impatiens* ('Little Lizzie')
Lois *Lotus hirsutus*
Lola *Viola*
Lori *Taxus baccata*
Lorna *Delphinium, Pelargonium, Viola*
Louisa *Hosta, Primula auricula, Viola*
Louise *Codiaeum variegatum, Diascia, Lathyrus odoratus, Nymphaea, Papaver orientale, Pelargonium, Streptocarpus*
Lucille *Fuchsia*
Lucinda *Camellia sasanqua, Fuchsia, Nerine, Pelargonium, Viola*
Lucy *Aster novi-belgii, Clematis* ('Lucie'), *Diascia, Lathyrus odoratus, Pelargonium, Thymus vulgaris, Viola*
Lulu *Lupinus, Tagetes tenuifolia, Viola*
Lutetia *Aster pyrenaeus*

Lydia *Dactylorhiza elata, Genista, Geranium, Viola*
Lyn *Coprosma petriei Streptocarpus* ('Lynne'), *Viola* ('Lynn')
Lynette *Streptocarpus, Syringa*
Lysander *Viola*

Madeleine *Chrysanthemum*
Madge *Viola*
Madonna *Antirrhinum, Dianthus, Gladiolus, Sambucus nigra*
Magda *Aquilegia vulgaris, Pelargonium*
Maggie *Primula auricula, Viola*
Mandy *Dianthus, Fuchsia, Streptocarpus*
Marcia *Rhododendron*
Marella *Sempervivum*
Margaret *Fuchsia, Primula auricula, Viola*
Margot *Lathyrus odoratus*
Maria *Begonia grandis, Dianthus, Nerine*
Marian *Viola*
Marianna *Saxifraga*
Marianne *Rhododendron* (azalea)
Marie *Calluna vulgaris, Hebe diosmifolia, Hyacinthus orientalis, Rhododendron* (azalea), *Sisyrinchium, Streptocarpus, Viburnum plicatum* ('Mariesii')
Marie-Louise *Viola*
Marietta *Schizostylis*
Mariette *Tulipa*
Marika *Viola*
Mariko *Rhododendron* (azalea)
Marjorie *Aster novi-belgii, Clematis montana, Hebe, Philadelphus, Phlox subulata*
Marilyn *Fuchsia* ('Miss Marilyn'), *Hosta, Pelargonium, Tulipa*
Marina *Erica cinerea, Malva sylvestris*
Marinette *Rosa*
Marion *Lathyrus odoratus, Pelargonium, Primula allionii, Sisyrinchium*
Marleen *Calluna vulgaris*
Mark *Primula auricula*
Marmaduke *Begonia*
Martha *Nymphaea, Rosa, Saxifraga*
Martin *Erica carnea, Primula allionii, Viola*
Martine Celery, *Rhododendron* (azaleodendron)
Mary *Fuchsia* ('Merry Mary'), *Nymphaea*
Mary Ann *Tulipa*
Mary Rose *Fuchsia, Rosa, Clematis viticella*
Matt *Hemerocallis*
Maureen *Astrantia major, Clematis, Fuchsia, Pelargonium, Streptocarpus, Tulipa*
Maxine Potato
Maya *Pelargonium*
Megan *Streptocarpus*
Melanie *Achillea millefolium, Calluna vulgaris, Fuchsia, Hebe,*

Nemesia, Pelargonium, Sempervivum
Melinda *Rosa, Viola*
Melissa *Begonia, Monarda, Pelargonium, Viola*
Melody *Calceolaria, Fuchsia* (and 'Golden Melody'), *Solenostemon*
Mercedes *Rosa*
Merlin *Epimedium* x *youngianum, Fuchsia, Galanthus, Nicotiana, Penstemon, Petunia, Pulmonaria, Rhododendron, Sempervivum*
Michael *Fuchsia*
Michelle *Pelargonium*
Micky *Delphinium*
Mimi *Rhododendron* (azalea), *Rosa*
Minerva Endive, *Viola*
Minty *Calluna vulgaris*
Mirabelle *Phlox*, potato
Miranda *Pelargonium, Phlox, Viola*
Mirelle *Calluna vulgaris*
Miriam *Primula auricula*
Modesty *Penstemon*
Molly *Pelargonium* ('Mollie'), *Rosa* ('Our Molly')
Mona *Viola*
Monica *Hebe, Primula auricula, Rhododendron, Viola*
Montgomery Brussels sprout
Morwenna *Viola*
Moyra *Fuchsia*
Muriel *Fuchsia, Geum* x *intermedium*
Myra *Rosa*
Myriam *Rosa*

❋

Nadia *Pelargonium* ('Nadja'), *Viola*
Nancy *Lamium maculatum* ('White Nancy'), lettuce
Naomi *Pelargonium, Viola*
Natasha *Calluna vulgaris* ('Natasja'), *Erodium* x *kolibanum, Clematis* ('Natacha') *Phlox maculata* ('Natascha'), *Viola*
Natalie *Erica carnea* ('Nathalie'), *Linaria, Pelargonium* ('Nathalie')
Neil *Hebe* ('Neil's Choice')
Nell *Clematis* ('Little Nell'), *Erica cinerea, Sempervivum, Tagetes triploid* ('Little Nell'), *Viola*
Nesta *Viola*
Nestor *Rosa, Veronica prostrata*
Nicki *Nicotiana, Cytisus* x *kewensis* ('Niki'),
Nicky *Pelargonium, Phlox paniculata*
Nico *Calluna vulgaris, Rhododendron*
Nicol *Dianthus*
Nicola *Fuchsia, Geranium*, potato, *Rhododendron* ('Nichola', azalea), *Streptocarpus*
Nicole *Cornus kousa, Viola*
Nicoletta *Rhododendron*
Nicolette *Fuchsia*
Nicolina *Fuchsia*

Nicoline *Chaenomeles* x *superba*
Nigel *Nymphaea, Primula auricula*
Nina *Viola*
Niobe *Aster novi-belgii, Clematis, Saxifraga, Sempervivum*
Noel *Pelargonium*
Nona *Viola*
Norbert *Sempervivum*
Norma *Primula auricula, Rhododendron* (azalea)

Octavia *Viola*
Olga *Callistephus, Clematis*, lettuce, *Rhododendron, Streptocarpus*
Olive *Rhododendron*
Oliver Brussels sprout, *Delphinium, Dianthus*
Olivia *Dianthus, Pelargonium*
Olwyn *Viola*
Olympia *Aquilegia, Verbena* x *hybrida*
Ophelia *Begonia, Rosa, Saxifraga, Verbena*
Oscar *Gladiolus, Pelargonium*

Paddy *Hedera colchica* ('Paddy's Pride')
Pamela *Aster novi-belgii, Lathyrus odoratus, Nymphaea, Viola*
Pandora *Delphinium, Fragaria* x *ananassa* (strawberry), *Lilium, Prunus, Viola*
Pascal *Pelargonium*
Patience *Fuchsia, Pelargonium, Primula auricula*
Patricia *Dianthus, Fuchsia, Geranium, Pelargonium, Rosa*
Patty Lettuce
Paul *Rosa* ('Paulii'),
Paula *Diascia, Saxifraga, Streptocarpus*
Pauline *Pelargonium, Primula auricula, Tradescantia* x *andersoniana*
Pearl *Lathyrus odoratus, Malus domestica* (apple)
Peggy *Lychnis flos-jovis, Primula auricula, Viola*
Penelope *Bougainvillea, Rosa, Saxifraga, Viola*
Penny *Pelargonium*
Percy *Kniphofia* ('Percy's Pride')
Peregrine *Paeonia lactiflora*
Persephone *Begonia*
Pete *Viola*
Petra *Calluna vulgaris, Saxifraga, Viola*
Petronella *Fuchsia*
Petsy *Sempervivum*
Phoebe *Aster pringlei, Hemerocallis, Lathyrus odoratus, Rhododendron, Viola*
Phyllida *Viola*
Phyllis *Fuchsia, Pelargonium*
Pia *Fatshedera lizei, Hydrangea macrophylla*

Pilar *Viola*
Pippa *Dahlia*, *Lavandula stoechas*, *Rhododendron* (azalea), *Viola*
Polly *Malus domestica* (apple)
Poppy *Viola*
Portia *Calceolaria*
Primrose *Begonia*
Priscilla *Gladiolus*
Prunella *Aster novi-belgii*
Purity *Aubrieta*, *Cosmos bipinnatus*

Rachel *Dianthus*, *Erodium*, *Heuchera*, lettuce, *Pelargonium*
Ramona *Primula*, *Rosa*
Randy *Magnolia*
Raphael *Paeonia suffruticosa*
Rebecca *Escallonia*, *Pelargonium*, *Viola*
Renate *Fuchsia*
Rex *Begonia*, *Saxifraga*, *Sempervivum*
Rhoda *Viola*
Richard *Daphne retusa* ('Richard's Choice'), *Populus alba* ('Richardii')
Ricki *Magnolia*
Rita *Juglans regia* (walnut)
Robbie *Fuchsia*, *Rosa*
Robert *Dianthus*
Roberta *Begonia*, *Dianthus*
Robin *Aquilegia*, *Daboecia cantabrica scotica*, *Leptospermum*, *Pelargonium*, *Pyrus communis* (pear), *Sempervivum*
Roger *Thuja plicata* ('Rogersii')
Roland *Miscanthus*
Romilly *Viola*
Ron *Fuchsia* ('Ron's Pet')
Ronnie *Sempervivum*
Rosabella *Arabis caucasica*, *Cornus kousa* ('Rosa Bella'), *Erica cinerea*
Rosabelle *Fuchsia* ('Rosabell'), *Rhododendron*
Rosalie *Consolida*, *Erica carnea*, *Heucherella*, *Hyacinthus orientalis*, *Pelargonium*, *Viola*
Rosalind *Calluna vulgaris*, *Lathyrus odoratus*
Rosamond *Clematis* ('Fair Rosamond'), *Lobelia erinus*, *Primula auricula* ('Rosamund')
Rosamunda *Fuchsia*, *Pelargonium*
Rosanna *Nymphaea*, *Sidalcea*, *Viola*
Rose *Aster alpinus*, *Gypsophila pacifica*
Rose Marie *Dianthus chinensis* ('Rosemarie'), *Fuchsia*
Rosemary *Primula auricula*, *Rosa* ('Rosemary Rose'), *Streptocarpus*
Rosie *Gaultheria mucronata*, *Hebe*, *Myosotis sylvatica*, *Solenostemon*
Rosina *Bellis perennis*, *Lathyrus odoratus*, *Rosa*
Rowena *Viola*
Ruby Brussels sprout, *Clematis alpina*, *Fuchsia*,

lettuce, *Rubus idaeus* (raspberry), *Streptocarpus*
Rudolph Broccoli
Rufus *Aster novi-belgii*, *Erysimum*
Ruth *Fuchsia*, *Helleborus foetidus*, *Sempervivum*

Sabrina *Delphinium*, *Saxifraga*
Saffron *Sempervivum*
Salina *Begonia*
Sally Endive, *Hedera helix*, *Primula auricula*, *Rosa* ('Sally's Rose'), *Streptocarpus*, *Viola*
Sally Anne *Galanthus* ('Sally Ann'), *Pelargonium*
Sam *Iris*
Samantha *Dahlia*, *Delphinium*, lettuce, *Pelargonium*, *Viola*
Samuel *Kniphofia* ('Samuel's Sensation')
Sandra *Hamamelis*, *Primula auricula*, *Streptocarpus*
Sandy *Verbena*
Sappho *Rhododendron*
Sarah *Geranium sanguineum* ('Sara'), *Kalmia latifolia*, *Lathyrus odoratus*, *Rosa*, *Streptocarpus*, *Viola*,
Sarah Jayne *Fuchsia*
Sasha *Pelargonium*, *Prunus avium*
Saskia *Rhododendron* (azalea)
Scarletta *Rosa*
Sebastian *Hemerocallis*
Selina *Diascia* ('Selina's Choice'), *Pelargonium*
Serena *Pelargonium*, *Viola*
Sharon *Pelargonium*, *Sempervivum* ('Sharon's Pencil')
Sheena *Aster novi-belgii*
Sheila Carrot, *Pelargonium*, *Primula auricula*, *Sempervivum*, *Viola*
Shelley *Pelargonium*
Sheri Anne *Rosa*
Shirley *Calluna vulgaris*, *Papaver rhoeas*, tomato, *Tulipa*, *Veronica* ('Shirley Blue')
Sian *Streptocarpus*
Siobhan *Fuchsia*
Sofia Courgette, *Dianthus*, *Rubus arcticus*, *Saxifraga*
Solomon *Delphinium*
Sonia *Aster amellus*, *Calluna vulgaris* ('Sonja'), *Dahlia*, *Helianthus annuus* ('Sonja'), *Lathyrus odoratus*, *Lobelia*, *Primula* x *pubescens* ('Sonya')
Sonny *Ficus pumila*
Sophia *Aster novi-belgii*, *Narcissus*, *Tagetes patula*
Sophie *Fragaria* x *ananassa* (strawberry), *Lathyrus odoratus*, *Osteospermum*, *Rosa* ('Sophie's Perpetual', runner bean, 'Sophy's Rose'), *Viola*
Stacey *Pelargonium*, *Rosa* ('Stacey's Star')
Stella Carrot, *Campanula isophylla*, *Diascia*, *Helianthus annuus*, *Primula*

auricula, *Prunus avium*, *Rhododendron*, *Rhodohypoxis*, *Saxifraga*, *Streptocarpus*
Stephanie *Calluna vulgaris* ('Stefanie'), *Erodium*, *Geranium*, *Nerine*
Stephen *Hedychium densiflorum*
Susan *Dianthus*, *Fuchsia*, *Halimium*, *Hebe*, *Primula auricula*, *Rhododendron*, *Rosa*, *Streptocarpus*
Susannah *Dianthus*, *Primula auricula*, *Viola* ('Susanah')
Susie *Campanula carpatica* ('Suzie'), *Narcissus* ('Suzy'), *Viola*
Suzanne *Phlox* x *arendsii*
Sybil *Iris*, *Viola*, *Philadelphus* ('Sybille')
Sylvia *Helleborus orientalis*, *Lathyrus odoratus*, *Tagetes patula* ('Silvia')
Sylvy *Fuchsia*

Tamara *Pelargonium*
Tamsin *Dianthus*, *Viola*
Tania *Camellia sasanqua* ('Tanya'), *Lobelia*
Tara *Hedychium*, *Viola*
Tatjana *Rhododendron*
Ted *Fuchsia* ('Our Ted')
Tess *Hedera hibernica*
Tessa *Delphinium*, *Kalanchoe*, *Rhododendron*
Thalia *Fuchsia*, *Narcissus*, *Viola*
Thelma *Viola*
Thea *Viola*
Theo *Dianthus*
Therese *Paeonia lactiflora*
Thomas *Dianthus*
Tiffany *Fuchsia*, *Magnolia*, *Narcissus*, *Pelargonium*, *Sempervivum*, *Viola*
Tim *Pelargonium*
Timothy *Kniphofia*
Tina *Erica tetralix*, *Sempervivum*, *Streptocarpus*, *Viola*
Titania *Delphinium*, *Dierama*, *Galanthus*, *Heuchera*, *Narcissus*, *Sempervivum*, *Viola*
Toby *Narcissus*
Tom *Viola*
Tommie *Helleborus orientalis*
Tony *Aster novi-belgii*, *Pelargonium*
Tosca *Aster novi-belgii*, cauliflower
Tracy *Pelargonium*
Tracey *Streptocarpus*
Trevor *Dianthus*
Tricia *Fuchsia*
Tristram *Narcissus*, *Sempervivum*
Trixie Broccoli, *Erica tetralix*, *Hebe*
Trudie *Pelargonium*, *Fuchsia* ('Trudy')

Una *Viola*
Unity *Pelargonium*, *Viola*
Ursula *Tagetes tenuifolia*

Valentine Cauliflower, *Fuchsia*, *Helianthus annuus*, *Pelargonium*, *Petunia*, *Rhododendron* (azalea), *Saxifraga*
Valerie *Fuchsia*, *Primula auricula*
Vanessa *Parrotia persica*, *Tanacetum coccineum*
Venetia *Saxifraga*, *Viola*
Venus *Aster* x *arendsii*, *Begonia*, *Crocosmia* x *crocosmiiflora*, *Nymphaea*, *Pelargonium*, *Senecio cineraria*, *Viola*
Vera *Clematis*, *Primula auricula*
Veronica *Pelargonium*
Verity *Hedera helix*
Vicky *Bougainvillea*, *Nerine*
Victor *Aster novi-belgii*
Victoria Celery, *Centaurea cyanus*, *Clematis*, cress, *Cyclamen persicum*, *Erica cinerea*, *Myosotis sylvatica*, *Passiflora* x *violacea*, *Pelargonium*, *Primula auricula*, *Primula* x *pubescens*, *Ribes uva-crispa* (gooseberry), *Salvia farinacea*, *Viola*, *Weigela*
Violetta *Aster novae-angliae*, *Aster novi-belgii*, *Browallia speciosa*, *Erica cinerea*, *Eryngium* x *zabelii*, *Pelargonium*, *Rhododendron* (azalea)
Virgil *Sempervivum*
Virginia *Lathyrus odoratus*, *Nymphaea*, *Pelargonium*, *Viola*
Vita *Viola*

Waldo *Rubus fruticosus*
Wanda *Aubrieta*, *Erica carnea*, *Primula*, *Viola*
Wendy *Agapanthus capaulatus*, *Chrysanthemum*, *Delphinium belladonna*, *Diascia*, *Fuchsia*, *Kalanchoe*, *Primula auricula*, *Saxifraga*, *Sempervivum*, *Veronica spicta*, *Viola*
William *Rosa* ('Royal William')
Willy *Clematis alpina*
Wilma *Cupressus macrcarpa*
Winifred *Fuchsia*, *Primula auricula* ('Winifrid'), *Primula* x *pubescens*, *Saxifraga*, *Streptocarpus*
Winona *Viola*
Winston Potato
Wynn *Hemerocallis*

Yolanda *Pelargonium*
Yvonne *Aster*, *Dahlia*, *Delphinium*, *Erica cinerea*, *Pelargonium*

Zara *Fuchsia*, *Hemerocallis*, *Viola*
Zaza *Sempervivum*
Zena *Pelargonium*
Zepherine *Viola*
Zoe *Pelargonium*, *Viola*

Index